P9-DFF-316

Praise for
If I Could Do It All Over Again

"Who of us would not wish that we could redo certain parts of our life? Or perhaps even all of it. Through this book, Jon Gauger is helping all of us to learn from one another and to gain insights into the lives of people who can help us. You will find *If I Could Do It All Over Again* a joy to read and filled with bits and pieces of wisdom, along with people's life experiences, that will help you on your journey. Read it, enjoy it, and share it with your friends."

Dr. Erwin W. Lutzer, pastor emeritus,
The Moody Church, Chicago

"All of us would like to reach back and recalibrate aspects of the way we have lived our lives. Jon Gauger introduces us to a variety of individuals who, looking in the rearview mirror, reflect on things they would do differently. These reflections serve to remind us of what's really important in life and to motivate us to live more productive and fruitful lives going forward."

Joseph M. Stowell, president,
Cornerstone University, Grand Rapids, Michigan

"Jon Gauger's many years as an on-air interviewer have enabled him to hone in on pertinent, insightful questions that have here produced responses from successful Christians that are transferable and applicable lessons to all readers. This book is a cornucopia of wisdom, advice, direction, and encouragement. Read it and grow!"

Dennis E. Hensley, PhD, author,
Jesus in the 9 to 5

"Six years of working closely with Jon Gauger have taught me to appreciate his passion for Christ and his creativity. And this book is no exception. In *If I Could Do It All Over Again*, Jon has used his amazing interview skills to get key evangelical leaders to share how they would answer some of life's most significant questions. Looking for a book that's fresh, insightful, and impactful? Then grab a cup of coffee, settle into a comfortable chair, and start reading *If I Could Do It All Over Again*. Life doesn't come with a 'Redo' button. But this book will help you learn from the experiences of others."

Dr. Charlie Dyer, host,
The Land and the Book radio program
Associate pastor, Grace Bible Church, Sun City, Arizona

"The questions we all would like to ask, Jon Gauger does ask! Just wait until you read the answers given by Tony Evans, Steve Brown, Josh McDowell, Michael W. Smith, and Joni Eareckson Tada to the question, What's one thing you can't wait to do in heaven?"

Jay Payleitner, speaker and bestselling author,
What If God Wrote Your Bucket List?

"Jon Gauger has given us a roadmap for the soul. If you want real-life wisdom and time-tested truth from people who have walked closely with Jesus, don't miss this book."

Chris Fabry,
author of *War Room* and *The Promise of Jesse Woods*

"This little book is filled with nuggets of practical and godly wisdom. If you were to have coffee with each of these great men and women, you wouldn't be able to gain anything more from their experience than what is captured right here. Definitely worth the read!"

Dr. Juli Slattery, clinical psychologist, author,
host of *Java with Juli* and cofounder of Authentic Intimacy

If I Could Do It ALL OVER Again

Jon Gauger

HARVEST HOUSE PUBLISHERS
EUGENE, OREGON

Unless otherwise indicated, Scripture quotations are taken from the New American Standard Bible®, © 1960, 1962, 1963, 1968, 1971, 1972, 1973, 1975, 1977, 1995 by The Lockman Foundation. Used by permission. (www.Lockman.org)

Verses marked NIV are taken from the Holy Bible, New International Version®, NIV®. Copyright © 1973, 1978, 1984, 2011 by Biblica, Inc.® Used by permission. All rights reserved worldwide.

Verses marked CEV are taken from the Contemporary English Version © 1991, 1992, 1995 by American Bible Society. Used by permission.

Verses marked NKJV are taken from the New King James Version®. Copyright © 1982 by Thomas Nelson, Inc. Used by permission. All rights reserved.

Verses marked KJV are taken from the King James Version of the Bible.

Cover by Koechel Peterson & Associates

Back cover author photo © Bethany Gauger

Cover photo © javarman / Shutterstock

IF I COULD DO IT ALL OVER AGAIN

Copyright © 2016 by Jon Gauger
Published by Harvest House Publishers
Eugene, Oregon 97402
www.harvesthousepublishers.com

ISBN 978-0-7369-6796-9 (hardcover)
ISBN 978-0-7369-6797-6 (eBook)

Library of Congress Cataloging-in-Publication Data
Names: Gauger, Jon, 1959- author.
Title: If I could do it all over again / Jon Gauger.
Description: Eugene, Oregon : Harvest House Publishers, 2016. | Description based on print version record and CIP data provided by publisher; resource not viewed.
Identifiers: LCCN 2016023961 (print) | LCCN 2015044108 (ebook) | ISBN 9780736967976 () | ISBN 9780736967969 (hardcover)
Subjects: LCSH: Regret—Religious aspects—Christianity. | Christians—Interviews.
Classification: LCC BV4509.5 (print) | LCC BV4509.5 .G38 2016 (ebook) | DDC 248.4—dc23
LC record available at https://lccn.loc.gov/2016023961

All rights reserved. No part of this publication may be reproduced, stored in a retrieval system, or transmitted in any form or by any means—electronic, mechanical, digital, photocopy, recording, or any other—except for brief quotations in printed reviews, without the prior permission of the publisher.

Printed in the United States of America

16 17 18 19 20 21 22 23 24 / ML-JC / 10 9 8 7 6 5 4 3 2 1

For Diana
If I could do it all over again, I would do it all over with you!

Acknowledgments

A writer is little more than a tangled ball of ideas whose on-target trajectory is reliant on the kindness of others.

To that end, I salute my wife, Diana. Before page 1 was written, she heard the dreams for this book. She lived through all the incessant chatter about interviews and edits, carefully reading every page. Through all of it, she has been a good sport. I love you, Princess Di.

Dan Anderson faithfully recorded most of the interviews featured in this volume. Chris Segard also assisted with several. Both of these guys have reliably supported me for years, and I am in their debt.

From the youngest age, my parents, David and Virginia, encouraged all six of their children to love God, work hard, and pursue dreams—never putting down my childish fancies. Thanks, guys!

For a long time, Dr. Robert Moeller encouraged me to write. Likely, this book would never have existed without his kindness and urging. Chris Fabry, Jerry Jenkins, and Jay Payleitner were also gracious with their encouragement. So was Colin Gray.

Moody Radio's Bill Davis and I spent many an afternoon carpooling on Chicago's Eisenhower Expressway. He pushed me to write—and doggedly followed up to make sure I did.

Dr. Dennis Hensley has proven to be a great writing mentor and friend. His first draft critique was invaluable.

Kim Moore of Harvest House first heard the idea for this book and believed in it, graciously walking me through the process. She is a model of Christian kindness. I thank her and Steve Miller.

Finally, thanks to the guests featured in this book, who courageously opened up their lives with a transparency that is at times breathtaking.

The sense of owing so much to so many is a humbling place to be. Thank you for sharing this journey with me.

Contents

Foreword by Joni Eareckson Tada

We've all done it. Somewhere along the line, you look in the rearview mirror of your life and wonder, *If I were given the chance, would I go back and do things differently?*

It's a question I'm often asked, except with a twist. "Joni, if you had the choice of not taking that dive, would you?" I know what they're getting at. Although nearly 50 years of living in a wheelchair with quadriplegia has its challenges, I've grown so much closer to Jesus through it. My prayer life and love for God's Word have deepened, and I lead a thriving global ministry to people with disabilities. Would I trade it all for the chance to walk? Perhaps at one time I would have leaped at the chance to run, skip, and jump. But now, many years later? I see God's wisdom in allowing my diving accident to occur. And I am *happy* with it.

That is not to say I would not go back and do things differently. There are plenty of times I have flubbed it, or missed golden opportunities, such as earning my college degree, for one. Mostly, though, I look in my rearview mirror and wish I would have invested more in my relationships and spiritual disciplines. I regret I did not cultivate more good habits. Alas, for me in my late 60s, it may be too late.

Or is it? Second Peter 3:8 tells us that God

looks at each day as "a thousand years." This means the Lord considers each day as our opportunity to invest in a thousand years' worth of eternal blessings. So even if I only have weeks left on this planet, every 24-hour slice of time *counts*! It is not—it is *never*—too late to change things; to pursue a dream, work on relationships, start new disciplines, or clean up old habits. And this is why the book you hold in your hands is so powerful.

If I Could Do It All Over Again is your chance to hear from some of the world's most respected and well-loved followers of Jesus, all of whom open their hearts to confess things they would have done differently...goals they wish they had pursued...or detours they regret taking. Their confessions provide sage advice and invaluable guidance for the reader. This book is your chance to learn from their misgivings and mistakes, as it were. As Job 32:7 says, "Age should speak; advanced years should teach wisdom" (NIV).

So flip the page and get started. And please, don't plow through *If I Could Do It All Over Again* too quickly. Get to know the heart of each contributor. Read their lessons prayerfully and act on their counsel intentionally. Get to the root of what you can add or subtract from your life, so you can move forward with Christ and learn how to invest more wisely in the days God gives you. Be a better believer for having walked with each contributor. And the really good news is, you don't have to break your neck to do it.

Joni Eareckson Tada
Joni and Friends International Disability Center
Agoura Hills, California

If Only I Had a Do Over

He was desperate, as few men ever are. Can you see him on his hands and knees, rocking back and forth? Hear his intense sobbing? Unearthly, really. Notice his fingers trembling as they trace the letters on the cemetery headstone beneath the creaking tree, his wide-eyed terror showing abhorrence at every touch. Now gaze upon his shoulders, sagging under the weight of his own wasteful life and behold the man: Ebenezer Scrooge. In literature or in pop culture, he has few equals for despair and regret.

If ever there was a man with an urgent need to do life over again, it was Ebenezer, the hard-hearted miser of *A Christmas Carol*. Dramatic life change evaded him until he was confronted by three ghostly visitors, each urging him to reverse his selfish ways. Even wrapped in the stilted words of Victorian English, Scrooge's climactic plea is wrenching: "Are these the shadows of things that *will* be, or are they shadows of things that *may* be, only?"

Pleading with the ghost of Christmas Future, the miserly Scrooge points out, "Men's courses will foreshadow certain ends, to which, if persevered in, they must lead, but if the courses be departed from, the ends will change. Say it is thus with what you show me!"

In a word, what Scrooge was asking for—begging for—is nothing more or less than what most of us occasionally dream of: a do over.

Do Overs

From our earliest days to our last moments, there resides within us all a soulish hunger to do life over again. Whether it's the Little League game we blew as a kid or a mistake made in the big leagues of life, we want another shot at it—whatever "it" may be. Inherent in our desire is the certain belief that if we somehow could get that second opportunity, we would definitely do better.

When I traded in my old smartphone for an upgrade, one of the apps I most looked forward to reinstalling was a bowling game I'd grown to love. I worked long and hard for my 181 average, and I was sure that with all the experience I'd had playing, I would surely increase that average—big time—with a fresh start on the new phone.

Want to know what happened? I bowled terribly. I didn't up my game—I ruined it. I was worse off with the new phone than before. So much for second chances.

In golf, when you take a horrible swing and the ball goes haywire, you get a mulligan, a penalty-free stroke replayed from the previous spot of the ball. It's as if the previous rotten shot never happened in the first place.

But wish as we may, real life rarely affords us a mulligan of any kind. There's no such thing as a fresh install in our past. Yet the desire for a second go-around is sometimes still with us. This wistful yearning of ours to take a second shot, to go back and make things right, is reflected in thousands of books.

Back in 1733, Samuel Madden penned *Memoirs of the Twentieth*

Century. Its pages unfold the story of a guardian angel who travels back to 1728 with letters from 1997 and 1998. Imagine the possibilities for a do over!

Television's most successful science fiction series, now more than a half century in the running, is the British cult phenom known as *Dr. Who.* The premise of the show is based on a humble-looking time machine known as the TARDIS, which transports Dr. Who to problems all across the time line of humanity. A recurring theme of the show is that somebody is in search of a do over, either to repair or prevent a disaster.

When it comes to Hollywood, the idea of going back in time to effect some kind of do over has long been a fascination of directors and screenwriters. It would be easy to compile a long list of films around this theme. There's...

A Connecticut Yankee in King Arthur's Court
The Time Traveler's Wife
The Butterfly Effect
Back to the Future (1,2,3)
Midnight in Paris
Somewhere in Time
Time Bandits
What If
The Time Machine
Time Crimes
Timecop
Planet of the Apes
Bill and Ted's Excellent Adventure
The Final Countdown

The Omega Man
Time After Time
Déjà vu
1984
Peggy Sue Got Married
Forever Young
The Terminator
The Philadelphia Experiment
Groundhog Day

What Christmas film has established more of a cult status than the beloved *It's a Wonderful Life*? When George Bailey is given a do over by way of a visit from his guardian angel, Clarence, his entire life is turned around. Instead of taking a suicidal jump off a bridge, he owns up to his challenges and embraces his life.

That's great for movies and books. But what about *real* life—yours and mine? I'm guessing you have one or two moments you wish you could do over. What's at the top of your list? If you could somehow repeat a scene or conversation, what's that singular moment that, with all your might, you wish you could somehow do over?

For me, it's not one thing, but many. Lots of my friends have a bucket list, but I keep a do over list. For instance, I would love to correct the disaster in junior high when we were playing flag football and a quarterback (who knew he was less than one second away from being pounded into the grass) threw to the only open receiver on the field—me. Grabbing the ball, I raced toward the end zone, virtually unopposed. It was only as I crossed the goal line that I finally understood the noise and yelling. I had run into my own end zone, scoring a nice touchdown for the *other* team! "Not such a big deal," you say. Actually, it was. That scene cast the mold of my unathleticism at an age in which doing well at sports meant the difference between thriving or dying in the junior high social world.

Then there was the halftime performance in high school when our marching band was executing all kinds of intricate formations out on the field. At a special moment in one particular song, all 96 of us were supposed to snap quickly around and march in the opposite direction (all of this captured on a movie camera up in the stands). I was the squad leader for our group of four, and I needed to pay extra close attention to the timing and execution of this maneuver. From the camera's vantage point high up in the press box, we musicians looked like a bunch of tiny but highly organized ants.

The movies were shown every Monday in band class as a visual report card on our weekend performance. These same images were shared at a special band concert at the end of football season, a sort of grand football farewell. There's a moment in this one particular movie where 92 ant-sized musicians flip around in one direction, while a squadron of four (my group) continue marching toward the wrong end zone! (Do you see a pattern here?) The only comedic relief was the sight of us four errant ants skittering to catch up with the other 92.

Of course, the older we get, the higher the stakes are, and the more serious our errors can become. The busy schedules of professional counselors, psychiatrists, and pastors offer further evidence of our hunger to redo scenes from our lives (or at least deal with the fallout from the fact that we can't). Trust me. I have plenty of adult-sized do overs I'd love to erase from my own list. I'm guessing you do too.

For some, do overs are big-ticket items: a divorce, a drunken spree, a fit of violence, flunking out of college, serving time in jail or at detox.

We wish these things were never, ever a part of our lives. Yet they are (forgiven, perhaps—but not without their natural consequences). Maybe your list is even darker. Or maybe it's much smaller (whatever *that* means—because in the end, all sin is equally sinful).

My contention is that with the passing of years, our greatest regrets may not be the big-ticket incidents—the major mess ups. Rather, I suspect most of us will come—like Scrooge—to regret the weight of the chain of *small* wrong decisions, *small* wrong attitudes we've indulged. In a moment of tender honesty, we might well confess to ourselves:

- I wish I had been more patient with my daughter/son/ spouse.
- I wish I had spent less time at work. I gave my soul to the company rather than to my family.
- I wish I had played more with the kids. They're gone now and have little time for me.
- I wish I had been a bolder witness rather than hiding behind the excuse that I don't have the gift of evangelism.
- I wish I had treated my parents with more respect—more gratitude. Now that they are gone, I feel guilty.
- I wish I had not been so adamant about watching my favorite television shows or all the box office hits, having little or no passion for spiritual disciplines.
- I wish I had been as faithful in praying with the body of Christ as I was about giving my body a workout at the health club.
- I wish I had learned what it truly means to "rightly divide

the Word of God"—instead of being satisfied with a lifetime of haphazard chapter-a-day Bible readings.

- I wish I would have gone on that mission trip when I was younger. I wonder now how much it would have shaped the direction of my life.
- I wish I wouldn't have dabbled in online pornography. Though I'm not a hard-core user, I walk around feeling dirty and ashamed.

I wish, I wish, I wish...If only our poor choices were like movie scenes on a set that we could somehow do over. Alas, we cannot. In retrospect, small bad decisions no longer seem so small. Or so few. They add up. Apart from the freedom that comes from a truly biblical worldview, our regrets link together like an ugly chain.

In *A Christmas Carol*, Scrooge's deceased business partner, Jacob Marley, appears before him, dragging a burden forged of rusty links. The clanking sounds accompany Marley's pitiful admission, "I wear the chain I forged in life...I made it link by link, and yard by yard."

What kind of chain are you lugging at this point in life? Just how long is it? How heavily does it weigh on you? We know that in Christ we are forgiven, yet we still hear the rattle of the chain. Is it possible our Christianity is warped?

Are you and I alone in this struggle? What about the leading Christian voices of our day? The Christian authors whom we read, the great musicians of our time, the pastors we hear on the radio...do they have regrets the same as we?

Do you ever wonder if famous Christians wish they could have a shot at a do over? After all, they are human like us. If so, what would *they* choose if they could do life all over again? And if there's a way finally to be rid of those ugly chains, what can we learn from these folks?

These are the very questions we're about to explore. We talked with a representative sample of some of the more well-known Christians of our time to ask—bluntly—"What would you do over again?" Before we're finished, we'll take a careful look at what we should do with the do overs we long for—but will never have—along with those regrets that never seem to leave us.

Make no mistake. This is a thoughtful book on a weighty subject. But don't despair! I promise by the time you're through reading, you'll have renewed hope, fresh courage, and the freedom you've been seeking from past mistakes.

A Word About Our Interviews

In putting together this book, I sat with a couple dozen of the more recognized names in the evangelical world as we know it today. To be considered for an interview, the subject had to be at least 50 years old (we're looking for the wisdom that only comes with time).

The comments you read are excerpts from actual conversations I conducted. Some of these conversations took place face-to-face. Most were recorded over the phone. Nothing is made up. Nothing is massaged or sugarcoated. These are real people sharing honest answers to some tough questions.

As you read, you may well ask, "Why didn't he interview my favorite Christian football player...or favorite Christian actor...or favorite Christian author or politician?" The answer is, with only so much time and only so many resources to devote to the project, we had to draw the line somewhere or this book could be thousands of pages long. And, to be frank, a few of the people we approached were simply uncomfortable addressing the kinds of questions we asked. So some of the names you may have hoped to see actually turned us down. Think of this book as a representative sample rather than an exhaustive collection of notable Christian voices.

That said, I hope you'll be touched by the sincerity and transparency you'll encounter. These are not easy issues to discuss in public. Perhaps, like me, you'll find yourself drawn as never before to the urgent encouragement in the imagery of Hebrews 12:1: "Such a large crowd of witnesses is all around us! So we must get rid of everything that slows us down, especially the sin that just won't let go. And we must be determined to run the race that is ahead of us" (CEV).

Let's allow the "crowd of witnesses" in this book to move us and motivate us toward a holier standard, a bolder witness, a larger faith, and a greater love for Christ. And as we commit to this journey, we may well join Tiny Tim in his invocation, "May God bless us—everyone!"

Contributor Biographies

Kay Arthur is the teacher and host of *Precepts for Life*, a daily television, radio, and online program that takes the student through the Bible book-by-book, verse-by-verse, using the inductive Bible study method. *Precepts for Life* has an audience reach of more than 75 million households, and it broadcasts into more than 30 countries.

Dee Brestin has written bestselling books and Bible studies stressing the need for friendship and female camaraderie in today's transitory society. Active in prison ministry, Dee is a frequent speaker at seminars and women's retreats, as well as a contributor to magazines such as *Focus on the Family*, *Guideposts*, and *Today's Christian Woman*.

Jill Briscoe is a British-American author, editor, and speaker. She has written or cowritten more than 40 books and serves as the founder and executive editor of *Just Between Us* magazine. As she travels the world with her husband, Stuart, Jill's vivid, relational teaching style has a unique way of connecting at the heart level.

Stuart Briscoe preached his first sermon at the tender age of 17. More than 65 years later, he continues to preach and teach the Bible. He served as pastor of Elmbrook Church near Milwaukee, Wisconsin, for 30 years. Stuart has written more than 40 books, ministered in more than 100 countries, and still preaches regularly around the world on radio and online through the auspices of Telling the Truth, a ministry he founded in 1971.

Steve Brown is a radio broadcaster, seminary professor, and the founder of Key Life Network. Among other titles, he authored *A Scandalous Freedom* and *When Being Good Isn't Good Enough*. Previously, Steve served as a pastor for more than 25 years and now devotes much of his time to the radio broadcasts *Key Life* and *Steve Brown, Etc.*

Michael Card has recorded nearly 40 albums, authored 25 books, hosted a radio program, and written for a wide range of magazines. His songs "El Shaddai," "Love Crucified Arose," and "Emmanuel" are among his 19 number one hits, and he has sold more than 4 million albums. *A Sacred Sorrow* was a Gold Medallion Award winner.

Gary Chapman is the *New York Times* bestselling author of *The Five Love Languages* (more than 8 million copies sold). Dr. Chapman speaks to thousands of couples nationwide through his weekend marriage conferences. He also hosts a nationally syndicated radio program, *A Love Language Minute*, and a Saturday morning program, *Building Relationships with Dr. Gary Chapman*.

Nancy DeMoss Wolgemuth has a love for the Word and the Lord Jesus that is infectious. These two loves permeate her online outreaches, conference messages, books, and two daily nationally syndicated radio programs—*Revive Our Hearts* and *Seeking Him*. Additionally, Nancy has authored 18 books, including *Lies Women Believe*, *A Place of Quiet Rest*, and *Seeking Him*.

Michael Easley is teaching pastor at Fellowship Bible Church, located outside of Nashville. A former president of Moody Bible Institute, Michael is heard on the daily 30-minute program *Michael Easley in Context*. He has written *Interludes: Prayers and Reflections of a Servant's Heart*, and coauthored *The Da Vinci Code Controversy* with Dillon Burroughs and John Ankerberg.

Tony Evans has served as the senior pastor of Oak Cliff Bible Fellowship in Dallas for nearly four decades, where he also serves as founder and president of The Urban Alternative. His daily radio broadcast, *The Alternative*, can be heard on more than 1000 radio outlets throughout the United States and in more than 130 countries. Dr. Evans is the author of numerous books, including *Kingdom Man* and *The Kingdom Agenda*.

June Hunt is an author, singer, and speaker. She is also the founder of Hope for the Heart. This ministry offers biblical counsel and coaching in more than 60 countries. Hope for the Heart's two popular radio programs are heard on nearly 900 radio outlets around the world. The author of many books, June has written *Counseling Through the Bible*, a Scripture-based counseling course.

Ron Hutchcraft has presented the gospel across North America and around the world, working with urban youth as well as Wall Street executives. Ron has spoken at NFL and Major League Baseball chapels, as well as Billy Graham pre-crusade events. His *A Word with You* radio broadcast airs on more than 1000 outlets in the U.S., Canada, and 15 other countries. Ron is also founder of the On Eagles' Wings ministry.

Tim Keller is the founding pastor of New York City's Redeemer Presbyterian Church, a ministry he started in 1989 with his wife, Kathy, and their three sons. Dr. Keller serves as chairman of Redeemer City to City, a ministry that starts new churches in major urban centers. Dr. Keller has written a number of *New York Times* bestselling books and is a sought-after speaker.

Anne Graham Lotz was called "the best preacher in the family" by her father, Billy Graham. Anne speaks around the globe with the wisdom and authority of years spent studying God's Word. Her *Just Give Me Jesus* revivals have been held in more than 30 cities in 12 different countries. Anne is also a bestselling and award-winning author.

Erwin Lutzer served for 35 years as senior pastor of The Moody Church. He is a celebrated international conference speaker and featured on two nationally distributed radio programs—*The Moody Church Hour* and *Running to Win*. Dr. Lutzer has authored more than 30 books, including *Hitler's Cross*, which won a Gold Medallion Award, and the bestselling *One Minute after You Die: A Preview of Your Final Destination*.

Gail MacDonald is an author, speaker, and counselor to women who live with leadership responsibilities. Gail has spent more than 50 years alongside her husband, who pastored four congregations before being named chancellor of Denver Seminary. Her books include *In His Everlasting Arms*, *The Heart of the Master*, and *High Call, High Privilege*.

James MacDonald has committed his life and ministry to the unapologetic proclamation of God's Word. In 1988, James and his wife, Kathy, planted Harvest Bible Chapel, which now ministers to more than 12,000 people at seven campus locations across Chicagoland. In addition to his preaching and writing ministry, James is heard on *Walk in the Word*, a Bible-teaching ministry on radio and television around the world.

Josh McDowell is one of the nation's foremost Christian apologists. He has spoken to more than 25 million people, giving more than 27,000 talks in 125 countries. Josh has written or cowritten more than 140 books, including *More Than a Carpenter* and *New Evidence That Demands a Verdict*. Josh's books have been translated into more than 100 languages, and four of his titles have received a Gold Medallion Award.

Bob Moeller is a "pastor to marriages" under the banner of For Keeps Ministries, cofounded with his wife, Cheryl. Previously a local pastor, Bob is an author of six books on marriage, two of which were nominated for the Gold Medallion Award. A conference speaker in demand, Bob has written articles for more than 150 publications, including *Focus on the Family* and *Marriage Partnership*.

Art Rorheim is a cofounder of Awana, International. This Bible memory program is found today in some 14,000 churches, orphanages, and Christian schools in more than 100 countries. Each week more than 1.5 million children and youth and 400,000 volunteers participate in Awana. In his nineties, Art continues to memorize the Scriptures and can quote entire books of the Bible.

Harold Sala pioneered the five-minute commentary in Christian radio. His long-running feature, *Guidelines,* is broadcast in 49 states and is heard the world over in a variety of languages. Dr. Sala, who holds a PhD in biblical text, has authored more than 55 books published in 19 languages. He speaks and teaches frequently at conferences, seminars, and churches worldwide.

Jan Silvious has been reaching out to women for more than 25 years, helping them to live fully in Christ. She's been a featured speaker at Women of Faith arena events and a plenary speaker for Precept Ministries' National Women's Convention and Moody's Women's Conferences. Jan is also a counselor and the author of a number of popular books.

Colin Smith serves as senior pastor of Orchard Evangelical Free Church. Born in Edinburgh, Scotland, Colin served as senior pastor of the Enfield Evangelical Free Church in London for 16 years before coming to America. Colin is the author of *The 10 Greatest Struggles of Your Life*, *10 Keys for Unlocking the Christian Life*, Unlocking the Bible Story Series, and *10 Keys for Unlocking the Bible*. He can be heard daily on the *Unlocking the Bible* radio broadcast.

Michael W. Smith has sold more than 15 million albums, scored 28 number-one hits, earned three Grammys, and received more than 40 Dove Awards. He is the founder of Rocketown, an outreach to young people. More than 800 teens from across the middle Tennessee region participate in programs each week at an affiliated high school after-school program.

Joe Stowell is an internationally recognized conference speaker and serves as president of Cornerstone University. He has written 20 books, including *The Trouble with Jesus, Following Christ, Simply Jesus and You, The Upside of Down,* and *Redefining Leadership.* Dr. Stowell also writes for *Our Daily Bread* and has hosted Christian historical film documentaries.

Joni Eareckson Tada became a quadriplegic at the age of 17, the result of a diving accident. Nevertheless, she went on to become the Founder and CEO of Joni and Friends International Disability Center, an advocate for people with disabilities. Joni has spoken in more than 47 countries and written more than 50 books. She is heard around the world through her radio broadcast, *Joni and Friends.*

 **George Verwer** is founder of Operation Mobilization, a ministry of evangelism, discipleship training, and church planting. George led Operation Mobilization for more than 40 years before transitioning to Special Projects for the ministry. Today OM reaches across the world through the ministry of their ship, *Logos Hope*. More than 6000 associates working in more than 110 nations make Christ known in the lives of all they meet.

 **Walter Wangerin, Jr.** is a *New York Times* bestselling author. Wangerin has won the National Book Award, the *New York Times* Best Children's Book of the Year Award, and several Gold Medallion Awards. In addition to his career as a writer, Wangerin served as an inner-city pastor in Evansville, Indiana, for 16 years. Today, he is senior research professor at Valparaiso University.

 **Ravi Zacharias** is founder and president of Ravi Zacharias International Ministries. Dr. Zacharias has spoken all over the world for 42 years at scores of universities, notably Harvard, Dartmouth, Johns Hopkins, and Oxford University. He has appeared on CNN, Fox, and other international broadcasts, and his own daily and weekly radio programs reach around the world. Dr. Zacharias has authored or edited more than 20 books, including *Why Jesus?*

What I Would Do More Of

I can still feel the wooziness. After 21 hours in the air, my legs felt like Jell-O, and staring at the rotating luggage belt—vainly hoping to find my suitcase—didn't help. Factoring in waiting time for the three flights to Luanda, Angola, we'd been traveling for nearly 36 hours.

As former Moody Radio Pastor Donald Cole led us out of the airport, I had nothing but a tripod and video camera with me. My suitcase never arrived. No aspirin. No bug spray as a defense against malaria-infested mosquitoes or prescription medication to prevent the dreaded disease.

Naturally, I'd packed my Bible in that now-lost baggage, so my daily quiet time became reciting verses I'd learned through the years. At first, this was comforting—enjoyable. But it didn't take long to exhaust my store of mental references.

In the darkness of an African night, I lay there overwhelmed with the sobering thought, *I wish I had memorized more—and longer—Scripture passages.* My mind wandered to stories of the persecuted church. What if I were imprisoned for my faith? Wouldn't surviving such an ordeal be much more likely if I could readily access the power of memorized Scripture? There is something profound about being confronted with that kind of loss. It shaped my life from that point on.

What about you? What if it were possible for you to repeat key scenes in your life? What would you choose to do *more* of?

For example, with the hindsight of years, I suspect most savvy investors would have put more money in select stocks they hadn't bought previously—maybe Microsoft. When the software company executed its initial public stock offering, a single share sold for $21. Let's say that back then you chose to buy a hundred shares. Twenty-five years later, your investment would have ballooned into 28,000 shares during the course of nine stock splits and be worth about $750,000. Could we somehow go back in time, we would surely invest more here (and in Apple Inc.!).

But what about other life arenas? What would you do more of— *much* more of—if you could do it all over again? It's interesting to hear what others have to say.

∽∽∽

Tony Evans

I would spend more time with my children. As a father, I'm certainly happy with how my children are doing, but I would have given even more time to my fathering because I see where there were some gaps I could have filled with more strategic time spent with them. Plus, I would have traveled a little less.

Ravi Zacharias

I would take more time out for fun things. For enjoyment, sports, recreation, and exercise, time with family, and time with my wife. All of these come into play. I would see a more balanced life than the ministry sometimes allows you to have.

Gail MacDonald

I have reached a new understanding regarding the power of prayer, but I wish I had come to this knowledge before I got to be in my seventies. I've been enjoying it for the past ten years. There is something very mysterious about the power of prayer, and it takes a quiet soul to get there. I tend to be a doer, and all my life I've had to work really hard at being a "be-er."

Dee Brestin

I would teach my children more memory work. I would have them memorize things like the *Shorter Westminster Catechism*. I read a lot to them, but I would read even more to them. When speaking, I would have spoken less about myself and more about Christ, so that my listeners' hearts would melt and their lives be transformed.

Anne Graham Lotz

I would like to have spent more time with my children when they were little, getting more involved in their schools. Also, I wish I had called my mother more, especially toward the end of her life. I didn't call her as much as I wish I had, and now I know the other side of that—how you long to hear from your children. Her life was full, but I wish I had talked to her more.

Michael Card

Clearly, I would have put in more time with my family. I think I was on the road doing 150 concerts a year for more than 30 years. My wife homeschooled our kids, so they received plenty of attention, and I would be home for two or three weeks at a time. I comforted myself by saying I was still spending more time with my children than my father, who was a doctor, ever spent with me because he was gone all the time. Yet my oldest son, Will, once took me aside in a non-condemning, sweet way and said, "I just need to tell you this. It was hard for you to be gone so much." I think that's one thing I would try to be wiser about.

POINT TO PONDER

Behold, children are a gift of the LORD,
the fruit of the womb is a reward.
PSALM 127:3

Gary Chapman

If I were looking back and asking where would I have spent more time, it would be in actually studying the Scriptures. As an associate pastor I regularly studied the Bible, and I consistently had a daily quiet time, but digging deeply into the Scriptures feeds the soul.

O how I love Your law! It is my meditation all the day.
PSALM 119:97

June Hunt

What would have made a huge difference in my life would have been to learn much earlier not to be manipulated. I needed to be less controlled by others. What helped me the most was Galatians 1:10, "Am I now seeking the favor of men, or of God? Or am I striving to please men? If I were still trying to please men, I would not be a bond-servant of Christ." Once I saw that Scripture, it began a process of change in me. The Word of God convicted me that I was allowing others to have undue control over me. At times, that control violated what I really believed was right. I needed to change—and coming to grips with that was a huge turning point for me.

POINT TO PONDER

Pray without ceasing.
1 THESSALONIANS 5:17

Ron Hutchcraft

I would invest a lot more time praying. I came late to understanding the power of prayer because I'm a doer. I think to those of us who are doers and "make-it-happen" people, prayer feels as if it's not as powerful as planning and doing and promoting and pushing and working hard and having vision and goals. However, it's the connection to the power of God to do anything! I've concluded that the amount of times I pray a day, the fervency with which I pray, and the desperation with which I pray (not necessarily bowing my head and closing my eyes, but consciously connecting with God), are measures of my dependency on God. The relational side, the intimate side of connecting with Him through prayer throughout the day, has come late in my life. Certainly, I would do more praying.

Bob Moeller

I would have invested more time in my friendships. Many men are prone to being loners, to being people who live life in a more solitary way. I tell people, "If you're wondering what to do with your time, consider the 'nursing home test.'" The nursing home test is this: 30, 40, 50 years from now when I'm confined to a nursing home and can't live independently any longer, who is going to come to see me? Is it going to be my business clients? Is it the people I was trying to impress? Who is going to show up and actually feed me when I can't do that myself? It's probably going to be my family, my kids, my grandchildren, my dearest friends. So, I think those who are going to be with you for the long haul, to the very end, deserve the best of your attentions.

POINT TO PONDER

A friend loves at all times, and a brother is born for adversity.
PROVERBS 17:17

Colin Smith

I wish I had settled core convictions of my ministry at an earlier stage of life. I'm very thankful for the theological education I had; it really taught me to think. But having been taught to think, I then had to settle through Scripture what I actually believed. In the early stages of ministry I found myself, at points, contradicting myself and my own preaching. I would see something from one text in the Bible and then see something different from another text, and I'd realize I was creating tension within my mind. What I needed was a more robust theological framework. If I had my time over again, I would pursue that at an earlier stage because it has been very significant for me.

Michael W. Smith

I'd invest more in people. When you're young, you're a little immature. You get excited about selling records, just getting a little selfish. I think if I had it to do all over again, I would invest more in loving on people and less in thinking about my desires and my comfort zone. Humility. Being more interested in the affairs of other people and what's going on. There's obviously not a lack of need. It's all around us. But it's amazing how you can become self-centered. I think I would have been much happier, and perhaps there would have been a lot more joy in my life, if I had learned earlier to love people for where they are at, being more concerned with their needs than my own.

George Verwer

I should have worked more on the area of patience and sins of the tongue. I thought I was working on this. I declared war on it and worked on it. But that's been my area of failure, where I've also hurt my wife at times. I'm just so quick to react.

Art Rorheim

I love sports—almost all of them. But I think of what God says in 2 Timothy 2:4, "No soldier in active service entangles himself in the affairs of everyday life, so that he may please the one who enlisted him as a soldier." I probably should have spent more time in my Bible and perhaps even more time memorizing Scripture, as much as I've loved it, and more time in prayer.

Joe Stowell

I would do more feeding of my soul. I wish I had taken more time—made time—(because we're all ultimately responsible for our own calendars) to read more. I would read more history, more biographies, more C.S. Lewis, more Muggeridge, a novel—to feed my soul and feed my mind. I find that as I look back, there's a shallowness that busyness creates. If I could do all of this again, I would take more time for meditation, just to sit for 20 minutes and say, "Lord, speak to me. Let me hear Your voice." I would take more time to reverse the ultimate shallowness that busyness threatens to bring.

POINT TO PONDER

Give heed to yourself and keep your soul diligently, so that
you do not forget the things which your eyes have seen and
they do not depart from your heart all the days of your life;
but make them known to your sons and your grandsons.

DEUTERONOMY 4:9

Erwin Lutzer

If I could do it all over again, I would spend an awful lot more time
investing in the lives of my children. Of course we prayed with them
and taught them and so forth, but in retrospect I really didn't enter into
their world as I could have. One day my second daughter, Lynn, wrote
me a letter when she was about to go into college. She said, "Dad, I cannot compete with your studies of Martin Luther and theology." Talk
about an ice bucket experience! Sure, I was studying Martin Luther,
and I was studying theology. But for my child to think that she couldn't
compete with that? That so set me back that I began to change my pri-
orities. I realized I was on the wrong track. If I could do it over again, I
would invest more in the lives of my children.

Parting Thought

The suitcase containing my clothes and Bible never showed up in
Africa—or anywhere. But that experience fueled a fire that continues to burn within me with regard to Bible memorization. I began

by creating a Scripture memory booklet. From there, I dove into the Psalms and memorized a dozen of those, and I'm still moving forward. Being middle-aged means I must commit to an aggressive schedule of maintenance and review of those passages or they disappear like the 10,000 neurons scientists claim my brain (and yours) loses every day.

Like you, and everybody we interviewed, I have a list of stuff I wish I'd done more of. The good news is that it's not too late to get to that list. God in His grace is using the loss in Africa to bring great gain to my life now. I'm convinced He can do the same for you too.

2

What I Would Do Less Of

The idea was doomed from the start. In a well-intentioned attempt at physical fitness, I agreed to play racquetball with my son, Tim, during my lunch break. I'd played as a student at Moody Bible Institute and also as a young married guy. Though I love the sport, it (apparently) no longer loves me. Tim and I discussed the fact that he is about half my age. We agreed we'd both "take it easy" and play "just a little bit."

Five weeks afterward, my throbbing back still reminded me I shouldn't have even attempted playing "just a game or two." No pill, heating pad, or massage regimen could ease the agony of my strained muscles. As of this writing, I have yet to return to the racquetball court.

It's one thing to overdo it in sports, but what about the rest of life? Given a moment of honest reflection, most of us could likely jot an uncomfortably long list of things we'd certainly do less of if only we could have a do over. You and I are not alone!

Joni Eareckson Tada

I would look at a lot less news on the television. I have to confess I'm a news junkie. When I go to the airport, I always stop by the news kiosk to pick up the latest edition of *Economist* magazine or *Newsweek*. I have to know what's going on in the world. That's not a bad thing. It's just that sometimes it becomes a fixation. It can depress my spirits. I mean, it's enough to know that there is an Islamic State where awful extremists are doing gross and detestable things in the name of Islam without having to hear another version on *CNN* or *ABC Nightly News* or the *PBS NewsHour*. That is why Psalm 101:3 is such a good verse for me: "I will set no worthless thing before my eyes." A television that is set to nothing but 24/7 cable news probably qualifies as a "worthless thing" for me.

Gail MacDonald

I would do a lot less hurrying. I've been a fixer, a person who loves to help. But in doing so, you have to deal with the fact that you may be missing out on the experience of "that calm soul." It was Dallas Willard who said, "Be ruthless with hurry." I've been working hard at this because as I age I realize I'm losing control of my body, my time, my future, my memories, and my influence. You have to deal with that in order to remind yourself that it's not about hurry. It's about the quiet, even though everybody else is doing the opposite. So I would do much less rushing.

Colin Smith

I'm surrounded by books in my office. The ones that make me smile are books that were topical and trendy in the 1980s but seem almost valueless now. In terms of my reading, if I could do life over again, I would spend more time with books of proven history—classic authors. I would pay much less attention to the books about vision and change (and whatever else was happening at that period of time). The press has produced a relentless amount of "the next new thing." Once you've been around for a few years, you look back at what was the next "new thing" (say in the 1980s), and it just makes you smile and say, "Why did I ever bother?"

Ravi Zacharias

I wouldn't worry as much. God is completely in control. Consider the emotional energy we spend pondering things, losing a night's sleep, or regretting certain thoughts we may have had or shared. As a Christian speaker, you worry that sometimes you may not have done as well preaching a sermon, so you toss in bed at night trying to recapture that moment. That is a draining thing, especially trying to relive a speaking experience. I would spend far less time worrying about all that and more time making sure those mistakes didn't happen.

POINT TO PONDER

Do not worry about tomorrow; for tomorrow will care for itself. Each day has enough trouble of its own.
MATTHEW 6:34

June Hunt

I would be less impacted by the opinions of others and continue to learn and grow and look at the opportunity to benefit others. I love learning, and I have viewed life as a fascinating journey. There will be times of failure, but this is no reason for me—or you—to keep beating ourselves over the head because of our failures. Years ago, a friend said to me, "June, you really don't know what grace is all about." I replied, "But I've taught on it!" She said, "Yes, but you don't have grace for *you*. You have grace for others." That was an eye-opener!

Tim Keller

I would do less surfing of the Internet, without a doubt. There are a hundred other things that would be better: more time with my wife, more time praying and meditating, more time reading. I think the Internet is a friend of information but an enemy of thought. It's great at snippets of information, but it doesn't help you think or reason. In fact, the more you're online, the less patient you are with sustained reasoning and with a longer narrative. It doesn't make you more able to think through critical issues. So I would certainly spend less time on the Internet.

Michael W. Smith

I'd be less concerned about "Are we selling records?" and "How many did we sell this week?" Less of that whole immature thing of trying to be recognized, trying to be accepted. It's amazing how you can get into that rut and base your whole life on what people think about you. There's really only *one* Person whose thoughts we need to consider, only one Person of whom we should be asking, "What is He thinking about?" It's Abba. We should be completely secure in that. But for a long time I didn't live this way. Again, I think that's just immaturity. So I would be less concerned about sitting out in the audience at a Grammy Awards night worrying, *Are they gonna call my name?* I would spend less time getting upset if they didn't. Looking back, I wish I had been just a little bit more mature.

Point to Ponder

You shall love the LORD your God with all your heart and with all your soul and with all your might.

DEUTERONOMY 6:5

Ron Hutchcraft

I would invest less effort in trying to make things happen and more in letting God make them happen. I am a doer, an aggressive person, and Psalm 37:5 has become an anchor verse for me: "Commit your way to the LORD." However, I find that after I've done that, I can slip a little bit and take it back—whatever "it" might be. But the verse goes on to encourage us, "trust also in Him and He" (HE, not me) "shall bring it to pass" (NKJV). I am not the Messiah. I don't have to fix everything. It isn't all up to me. So I would do more praying, more depending on God, more waiting on God, and less trying to make things happen.

James MacDonald

I would invest less conversation in trying to persuade people about matters of personal change. Whether it's a couple going through a marriage crisis or a staff member working at less than his full potential, I have found through the years that people respond to grace. People respond to patience and kindness. I have been spectacularly dissatisfied with my capacity to change the behavior of others through conversation.

George Verwer

I would watch fewer movies. I think some of the films I watched were definitely a waste of time. But the main thing I would like to do less of is sin!

POINT TO PONDER

Take diligent heed to yourselves to love the LORD your God.
JOSHUA 23:11

Tony Evans

I love sports. I love watching sports and keeping up with sports. But I would probably spend a little less time on sports if I could do it all over again. Plus, I would have traveled a little less.

I would be less critical of other people. The older I get, the more I realize I haven't lived other people's lives. I haven't been through what they have been through. Had that been the case, I may have done things a whole lot worse than they did. I think that being critical of other people—finding their faults and seeing their shortcomings—is often just a way of covering our own insecurities, our own lack of confidence or contentment with our lives. Instead of being critical, I would commit to finding the value, the virtue, and the redeeming aspects of any individual—even the difficult ones. In the end, that creates a much more loving example for children and others to see. Someone once said, "When you don't know what to do, you can always choose kindness." How true!

~~~

Parting Thought

In a culture that practically screams, "Do more!" the notion of doing less is tough to embrace. We are driven—and proud of it. Yet, ironically, for most of us, the only way to *be* more for Christ is to do less of _____. I cannot fill in the blank for you, any more than you can for me.

This much I know. The only way we can do more of truly worthwhile things with our family, church, friendships, ministry, and job is by consciously—repeatedly—choosing to do *less* of other things. Let's not be so naive as to think that doing less of those things won't cost us. It will. But in the end, choosing only those things that magnify Christ in us will yield the least regrets.

Let's take for our personal vision statement the humble words of John the Baptist, who said of Jesus, "He must increase, but I must decrease" (John 3:30).

Here's to living a life that proves "less really is more"!

3

Why Can't I Do Better?

Forgive me, basketball fans. I am about to offend you. Should you wish to issue a technical foul for my forthcoming conduct, I will surely understand. Yet I do have a complaint against the hoopla surrounding hoops: too many missed free throws.

The average NBA game offers 26 free throw opportunities. Apart from the pressure that comes from playing in any sport, the extremely well-paid NBA players face no significant variables in shooting a free throw. There is no wind to blow the ball off course, no extreme temperature that might freeze the athlete's fingers or adversely affect ball grip. Players do not worry about the sun in their eyes or an odd placement of the ball (unlike a field goal kicker in the NFL) or variations in distance (again, unlike football). Nor is the clock much of a factor.

Want to know how many of those precious points are blown in a typical game? Seven. Just 19 out of 26 free throw shots are successful in an average NBA game. That means nearly 27 percent of all free throws are missed. If I missed 27 percent of anything in my job, it would not go well for me. I would be kicked off the team!

So why, despite experience that goes back to childhood pickup games, despite knowing the basket is 15 feet from the free throw line—every time—do NBA players miss so many free throws? Said another way, why can't they do better? No one seems to know.

I wonder the same question about life as a whole. Why can't we do better? I suspect that just like at the free throw line, we are so accustomed to missing so many opportunities, it rarely strikes us as odd—let alone wrong—that we mess up as much as we do.

Consider that as followers of Christ in the twenty-first century, most of us have Bibles on our shelves, Bibles on our smartphones, Bibles (even audio Bibles) on our tablets. We have unparalleled access to commentaries, Greek and Hebrew language tools, sermons, devotionals, and Bible studies.

More than this, we enjoy the unique status of having the wisdom of Augustine, the passion of Luther, the pen of Bunyan, the brilliance of Spurgeon, the boldness of Bonhoeffer, and the combined experience of believers that stretches across two millennia.

Why, then, do we make so many of the same mistakes, fall for the same traps, and get caught in the same sins as our forebears? The question touches equally on issues of theology, history, and human nature. Why can't we do better?

Stuart Briscoe

I think we *do* do some things better, but we're never going to get them completely right. The old business of being created in the image of God, but fallen, is a fundamental aspect of our humanity. We're going to have to recognize we are on a steep learning curve. We learn slowly at times, and we frequently do not take to heart the lessons of previous generations or even from our personal experience. I wouldn't say we don't learn from history. We don't learn *enough* from history. Or we don't implement enough of what we've been learning.

Michael Card

I recently heard somebody say that what we learn from history is that we *don't* learn from history. I think that's partly because of the fall. The fact that I'm fallen and fragmented internally means I habitually say and do the wrong things. Even people with good intentions often end up doing the wrong things. That's just part of the fall.

POINT TO PONDER

No temptation has overtaken you but such as is common to
man; and God is faithful, who will not allow you
to be tempted beyond what you are able,
but with the temptation will provide the way of escape also,
so that you will be able to endure it.
1 CORINTHIANS 10:13

Tony Evans

I think one of the reasons we don't leverage lessons from the past is because we face a spiritual enemy. He knows our weaknesses individually, and he can attack them individually. So while we may have heard something yesterday, from our parents, or from the past (you see this in the Bible too), people make the same mistakes. We are under a fresh attack. The freshness of the attack assaults us in a direct way. The reality is, having yesterday's knowledge doesn't necessarily transfer to the fresh attack of today.

Ron Hutchcraft

We're stubborn, and we are all the product of our own experiences. We've seen how our parents do things and how other people do things "in ministry" instead of copying the Lord's example. Actually, we are a lot better at studying His Word and knowing His Word than *doing* His Word. It seems that something breaks down when you and I fall into one of life's tricky situations. Typically, we struggle working it through in a biblical way. It's as if we have compartmentalized life: "Here are the verses...here are my choices..." Somehow we have not let the verses get into the choice compartment.

June Hunt

With children, more is caught then taught. So often we think, *If my father was this way, that's what it must mean to be a husband, a father, a man.* Or, *My mother was this way, so that's what it's supposed to be like.* These help form patterns in our home. But I have come to learn that often my sense of normal was (and is) not normal! Maybe what *your* normal was is not normal. But we don't grasp that. Consequently, every generation has to learn this. We learn from experience that there might be a better way than the one we chose.

POINT TO PONDER

Fathers, do not provoke your children to anger,
but bring them up in the discipline and
instruction of the Lord.

EPHESIANS 6:4

Steve Brown

We like to sin! We like to sin because of what Adam and Eve did and because of the fall. We wouldn't sin if we didn't like it. So we make choices—bad choices. Here is the reason for the cross. If we could do better, God would have sent us a really nice book and said, "Here's the book. Just go to it." But obviously our problem was bigger than that. So He sent His Son to die on a cross in our place. You can tell how big a problem is by what it takes to fix it. In our case, it took the blood of God's own Son to fix it. So we must have a bigger problem than merely "do better"—a *much* bigger problem than just "do better," given the sacrifice of Christ.

POINT TO PONDER

This is the judgment, that the Light has come into the world,
and men loved the darkness rather than the Light,
for their deeds were evil.

JOHN 3:19

Michael W. Smith

We are in desperate need of a Savior, aren't we? You would think we would learn. But the good news is there is hope. I like whom I'm becoming, if I can be so bold as to say that. Every night I share that with people at my concerts. I tell them, "If you can't go home and look at the mirror and say to yourself, 'I like whom you're becoming,' then I'm not sure you have the grace thing figured out yet." So I find a lot of hope, actually. But we do seem to take our time learning life's lessons, probably a little longer than we should.

Nancy DeMoss Wolgemuth

We can learn much from the lives of others. That's one reason I love reading biographies of people who walked with the Lord and who served Him. I love reading about their successes and their failures and then pondering, *What is there about their example that is worthy of being followed? What choices or mistakes did they make I want to avoid?* I also enjoy reading in the Scriptures about the lives of those who have walked with the Lord or *not* walked with the Lord. I learn from their examples, from their cautions, from the outcome of their lives. That's what the writer to the Hebrews says: "Remember those who led you, who spoke the word of God to you; and considering the result of their conduct, imitate their faith" (Hebrews 13:7). But, ultimately, we're not to put our focus on *them*. Instead, remember Christ. He is the One who is the same yesterday, today, and forever. It's by fixing our eyes on Him that we become who He made us to be.

Erwin Lutzer

I think the reason we don't do better is because we as human beings have to learn on our own. How many of us as children always obeyed our parents? The fact is, we didn't. But along the way, perhaps we learned that obeying was a very good idea. I think you can warn young people (just as we've been warned), yet the ways of the flesh are still often followed rather than the ways of wisdom. So we have to learn the same old lessons again and again.

Point to Ponder

Oh, the depth of the riches both of the wisdom and knowledge of God! How unsearchable are His judgments and unfathomable His ways!

ROMANS 11:33

James MacDonald

I think issues of personal holiness are learned again and again from generation to generation. We need to learn that when God says, "Don't," He means, "Don't hurt yourself." When God tells us to do something, all that He commands, He commands for our blessing. All that He forbids, He forbids as a protection. It seems that everybody has to learn that from generation to generation. On the other hand, I believe we have made progress in the doctrinal formation of the church through the centuries. In our era, the inerrancy of Scripture was hammered out. There was the generation that settled the deity of Christ, and defined what the church is. So I think that while we do progress in terms of our understanding of biblical doctrine, we seem to need to go through the same cycles—every generation—to learn about personal holiness.

Gary Chapman

To me, one of the key issues in whether we repeat history or whether we learn from history is whether we *know* history. If people read and know something about what's happened in the past—whether we're talking about biblical history or secular history—the less likely they are to repeat the mistakes of the past. Instead, we will be more likely to build on it and make better choices, which I think is what God intends. We've done that when it comes to knowledge—technical knowledge. Look at all the things we know today that we didn't know 50 or 60 years ago. So we have built effectively on history when it comes to technical knowledge. But, unfortunately, we haven't done that well when it comes to things such as character and living moral lives. I wish we would expose our children to more history, both Christian and non-Christian history, so that they *can* build upon what has happened rather than repeat it.

Bob Moeller

I think the reason we don't do better is pride, perhaps more than anything else. The Bible says, "There is a way which seems right to a man, but its end is the way of death" (Proverbs 14:12). Inborn in our fallen nature is the idea that we know best. Even though others have said to do differently, our thought is, *What do they know?* or *They haven't lived my life*, or *They don't understand the things I understand*. At the end of the day, I think the decisions I made that I would make differently now (if I could go back into the past) were influenced an awful lot by pride. With age comes humility (if you're letting God work in your life). As the years go by, He humbles you. The Bible says that God "is opposed to the proud, but gives grace to the humble" (1 Peter 5:5). Part of that grace is to learn from our mistakes and to learn from the mistakes of others.

POINT TO PONDER

Let him who thinks he stands take heed that he does not fall.
1 CORINTHIANS 10:12

Joe Stowell

We're all fallen, we're all twisted, and we all struggle with the same deficiency that the fall of Adam and Eve has brought into our lives. Plus, we're driven by the pressures, the temptations, and the seductions of the present. So when you combine our frailty and our fallenness with the pressure of the moment, I don't think any of us are going to say, "Let me just go back and read that history book, that biography about whoever did better in a moment like this." Nor will we take the time to process, "What about Moses? You know, I wonder what he would do in a moment like this." In the fast-paced crush of life, I think we're often our own worst enemies. The important thing is to grow personally from failures. Whereas we may not learn from the past, we need to learn from our own present: to process what we did and why we did what we did. Then we need to confess. "Okay, I've been reminded again of my own frailty. This battle I've just lost is a particular weakness, and by God's grace I'm going to memorize verses that address that. I'm going to be much more aware the next time that thing starts coming at me." To grow like this would be the best thing we could do.

Kay Arthur

Too many people are not in the Word of God on a daily basis. They may be reading devotionals written by other human beings, with a verse or two inserted in the daily text, but they are not face-to-face with the Bible, hearing, learning, and absorbing what God says. Therefore, they don't know truth: who God says He is, what is right, what is wrong, how to correct it, how we are to live. Jesus told us that truth sets us free (John 8:32).

∾∾∾

Parting Thought

This question of why you and I can't do better is not new. Paul himself expressed a similar frustration when he wrote in Romans 7:19-20, "The good that I want, I do not do, but I practice the very evil that I do not want. But if I am doing the very thing I do not want, I am no longer the one doing it, but sin which dwells in me."

Sin is the reason. Sin is why we cannot do better than we do. Sin has lots of names, wears lots of hats, is disguised a thousand different ways. Yet sin is still sin.

If sin is the reason we struggle so much in trying to do better, what is the solution? Paul offers a generous slice of hope later in the passage:

> Wretched man that I am! Who will set me free from the body of this death? Thanks be to God through Jesus Christ our Lord! So then, on the one hand I myself with my mind am serving the law of God, but on the other, with my flesh the law of sin (Romans 7:24-25).

If you and I are going to have fewer regrets looking back at the end of life, it will surely be the result of a realistic assessment of sin—and a grand vision of the One who conquered it.

Thanks be to God!

4

A Life Lesson I Will Never Forget

The scar is still there. May I tell you how I got the thing?

It was the Friday before Labor Day, and I was in a hurry to catch the train from downtown Chicago to our home in the suburbs. The minivan was packed, and the second I arrived we would head out to our favorite camping spot.

My daily commute from Moody Bible Institute to the train station requires a mile-and-a-half walk, which I take at a brisk pace as it is virtually the only exercise I get. Call it competitive walking (meaning I get mildly ticked off if I see someone walking faster than me).

Throughout the years I've learned the shortcuts involved in walking as the crow flies. At one point, I step over a guardrail, snake across a parking lot, and then cross a bridge over the Chicago River. On one "walk to remember," I failed to make sure my foot cleared the guardrail.

Falling headfirst over the barrier, my feet flew up high in the air. Involuntarily, I kicked downward in a too-little-too-late attempt at righting my body. That downward kick thwacked my shin against the edge of the guardrail with the force of a hurtling piano (at least it felt that way).

First came the stabbing feeling, and then a sour stomach. Was the leg broken? Shin cracked? There was no time to indulge the pain, and I really didn't want the delay of a possible doctor visit to slow down or derail our camping weekend.

So I carefully got up, put some weight on the leg, and was pleasantly surprised that it didn't buckle beneath me. Just a few blocks later, I staggered onto the train, exhausted. Rolling up my pant cuff, I finally surveyed the damage: bloody, ugly, but not broken.

If I live to enjoy a full century of competitive walking, I promise you I will never forget that wretched fall—or fail to look before I take the big step over any parking lot guardrail. Call it a life lesson.

Wonder what some well-known Christians would call a life lesson? Let's find out.

∽∽∽

Michael W. Smith

I could go ten different places in talking about life lessons, but my gut tells me the greatest life lesson I have found is in watching my dad love my mom and cherish her. I say that because I've been married for more than 30 years, and I learned a lot about how to treat my wife and how to respect her by watching my dad respect and love my mom.

Gary Chapman

I think the biggest lesson I have learned through life—and one I continue to be aware of—is centered on what Jesus said in the Gospel of

John, "Without Me you can do nothing" (John 15:5 NKJV). I remember when I graduated from college, I had the idea, *I'm a college graduate. I can do whatever needs to be done. Turn me loose!* My first assignment was working in a print shop running a folding machine. For two weeks, I gave it everything I had for eight hours a day, but I couldn't get that folding machine to work. One morning in my devotional time I read in John 15:5, "Without Me you can do nothing." That's when it finally hit me, and I just said, "God, without You, I can't even run a dumb folder!" I have never forgotten that lesson. Apart from God, I can do nothing.

Jan Silvious

Life lesson: "What might have been does not exist, so don't even go there." I know a lot of people who live in regret, and they live in what-might-have-been: "If only I had done this, if only I had done that." That thinking takes us nowhere. Because what-might-have-been doesn't exist, why do we even try to visit? I have learned to look at my life in the past and simply say, "You know, what might have been does not exist." Thinking about those moments takes us down every time. Let's not go there!

Erwin Lutzer

My mother once told me that when I was a baby sleeping in the crib, the pastor who had performed my parents' marriage came over for a visit, along with his wife. Before she left, the pastor's wife leaned over in the crib, gave me a kiss, and said in German, "He will be the preacher."

I don't know whether or not she spoke offhandedly or whether she was inspired by the Holy Spirit, but the fact is her prediction came to pass. As I look back on my life, I see the providence of God everywhere. There were decisions I made that I thought at the time had no special significance, but in looking back, I see nothing but the providence of God in my life as He guided me in destiny decisions when I thought they were just small, offhanded choices.

POINT TO PONDER

How precious also are Your thoughts to me, O God!
How vast is the sum of them! If I should count them,
they would outnumber the sand.
When I awake, I am still with You.
PSALM 139:17-18

Anne Graham Lotz

When I was 17, I attended a training institute in California and felt bound by what other people expected of me, people who thought I wasn't what Billy Graham's daughter ought to be. But somebody said to me, "You're looking at God through a prism—these other people. You need to look at God directly." From that point on, the summer of my seventeenth year, I made the decision to live my life to please an audience of One. I knew if God was pleased, my parents and grandparents—the people I cared most about—would also be pleased with me. Some people wouldn't be, but you can't please everybody anyway.

I live my life 24/7 in utter devotion to please the Lord. I'm not saying I please Him all the time, but that's my aim.

Nancy DeMoss Wolgemuth

One of the most formative lessons in my life is one my parents taught me when I was a little girl: God is the Supreme Ruler of all things. Everything He does is good and wise and just and holy. That truth came to bear in my life in an unforgettable way on the afternoon of September 1, 1979, when having just left my parents after spending a weekend with them on my twenty-first birthday, I'd gone back to my home in Virginia. I got a call saying that in the few hours since I had last seen my dad, he had a heart attack and was instantly with the Lord. At that moment, all those things my dad had taught me for the first 21 years of my life came back to me like a flood. The verse that immediately came to mind was Psalm 119:68 that says (paraphrased), "God is good and everything He does is good." In the midst of the tears and the huge sense of loss and grief that followed, there was this underlying, bedrock assurance that God is good, and everything He does is good. That was more than 35 years ago, and I would still say that the foundation of my life, the thing I come back to again and again and again, is that God can be trusted. Heaven rules! He is faithful! He is true! He can be trusted.

Stuart Briscoe

I haven't graduated from the School of Hard Knocks. I seem to be stuck in second grade and keep having to redo it! But I would say one of the huge life lessons I have learned is that ministry requires three things of me: First, I must preach the Word. Secondly, I must love the people. Thirdly, I must trust that the Spirit will move. Those are the three dimensions of the huge life lesson I've learned—and I still am learning.

POINT TO PONDER

I do not consider my life of any account as dear to myself,
so that I may finish my course and the ministry
which I received from the Lord Jesus,
to testify solemnly of the gospel of the grace of God.

ACTS 20:24

Tony Evans

A life lesson for me? It's the power of grace. Grace can do for me what I can never do for myself. We are so self-sufficient that we will often trump what God wants to do with our own will. Maybe we will be successful to some degree, but it will be a success with frustration and irritation and aggravation. Whereas through grace, which is what God does for us, He lets things flow. And they flow very naturally without stressing. I wish I would have leaned more on that rather than trying to force stuff to happen.

Ron Hutchcraft

I think one lesson I have learned is that God is always doing something bigger than what I can see in front of me. I thank Him even for the mistakes and for the wrong turns. I thank Him for His great faithfulness because He has been weaving a tapestry that you only begin to see as you follow Him faithfully for many years. Right now we see only the threads. But as you progress further, you begin to say, "Wow! Look at what happened back when I was just 13. It's still important right now. God is using that experience right now! I had no idea back then." All of that gives me courage to say, "I'm only seeing the threads today, but they are part of this great master tapestry."

POINT TO PONDER

Do not call to mind the former things,
or ponder things of the past. "Behold, I will do something
new, now it will spring forth; will you not be aware of it?
I will even make a roadway in the wilderness,
rivers in the desert."
ISAIAH 43:18-19

James MacDonald

Just because God calls person "A" to be passionate about something does not mean that person "B" should be passionate about the same thing. I can remember guys coming up to me after church, and they would say, "Man, we are so fired up about this inner-city mission" or "We are so excited to be going as missionaries to Bolivia." That was their life passion, which was great. But many of these folks were shocked when other people weren't as passionate about their goal as they were. This is a life lesson I had to learn. The main thing is to be passionately engaged in the work of God's kingdom. Romans 11:29 points out, "The gifts and the calling of God are irrevocable." We should fully engage in the thing that the Lord has led us to do but not feel the need or even be disappointed when others are directed to do different things.

Dee Brestin

When I understood I had made the issue of control a personal heart idol, I suddenly realized why I had trouble keeping administrative assistants. I always thought it was "her fault." *What is the matter with this woman? This is a great job! I pay her well. It's exciting, it's ministry, it's travel.* But it wasn't until I was lamenting to my friend Jan Silvious, and she said, "Seems to be a pattern in your life," that I woke up. I began a study of heart idols and understood I had a problem with control. I was manipulative, and God opened my eyes.

Art Rorheim

The life lesson I will take to my grave is that I want to always share the clear message of the gospel. We are now living in a day like Paul lived in. In Galatians 1:6-7, he says, "I marvel that ye are so soon removed from him that called you into the grace of Christ unto another gospel: Which is not another" (KJV). Paul saw how they were moving away from the essentials of Christianity, and it broke his heart. I find today that the biggest challenge I have working with Awana—or wherever I am—is to give the clear message of the gospel. The gospel is not an exchange program where God says, "I'll give you eternal life if you'll give Me your life." We have nothing to give because dead people cannot give anything! We are dead in trespasses, and we can't give a thing until we get life, until we get eternal life. Then we give everything we've got. So that's the thing I want to take to my grave—to be God's witness.

Jill Briscoe

When I was studying the names of God, somewhere I read that one of God's names means "I will be all you need Me to be when you need Me to be all that you need." Of course, this speaks of His total self-sufficiency. For me, the life lesson has been the challenge of learning how to stay close and draw on the power, blessing, comfort, strength, and inspiration of the Spirit. When I've done that, He's been all that I've needed Him to be when I've needed Him to be all that I've needed. Life lesson!

POINT TO PONDER

"Do you not fear Me?" declares the LORD.
"Do you not tremble in My presence?"
JEREMIAH 5:22

Colin Smith

When I think about the hardest time I went through in ministry, there were really three life lessons that came out of it. Lesson one is don't try to defend yourself. You can't do it. You have to leave that to the Lord and to others. A second lesson is always try to speak well of others. The third lesson is from Hebrews 12:15, "See to it that no one comes short of the grace of God; that no root of bitterness springing up causes trouble." These three lessons have served me well and are wise principles for all of life.

Michael Easley

Cindy and I had been married just a few months when we were invited to a party at a doctor's house. We were all talking and eating, enjoying ourselves, when someone struck up a conversation, and I mentioned we'd just gotten married. I then made some quip like, "You know, I guess if it doesn't work out we could always get a divorce." The doctor hosting the dinner immediately walked me back to his office. His eyes were aflame, his temples were bulging, and he got within an inch of my nose. He said, "Don't you ever joke or tease about divorce again!" I said, "Okay, Doc, I get it." He said, "No, you don't! Don't ever use those words again!" Let me tell you, I heard it. More than 30 years later I still remember it. I wish a lot more people like that were willing to get in a lot more young couples' faces and yell at them and say those kinds of words.

Michael Card

When I was a kid, I often sat in church next to an old man named Basil Edwards. I remember that when I was seven years old, I got into trouble and was crying. Basil got on his knees, face-to-face with me. He said, "Mike, I want you to know you're wrong. What you did was wrong. But I want you to know I'm on your side, right or wrong. In fact, *especially* when you're wrong, I want to be on your side." I think what I will take to my grave is that was the first time I ever really understood the gospel. Because while we were sinners, Jesus said, "I'm going be on your side." Before there is any hope or indication we will repent and come to Him, Jesus still stoops and, essentially, gets face-to-face with us and says, "You're wrong, but I'm going be on your side." Many years later I had a son who had been arrested a couple of times for smoking pot. Every time I'd go to court with him, I would say, "What you did was wrong, but I want you to know I'm here because I'm on your side. Right or wrong, I choose to be on your side. You need to know that." Later, after he turned his life around, my son called me and said, "That was the gospel, Dad, wasn't it?" I said, "Yep. Absolutely."

POINT TO PONDER

We also once were foolish ourselves, disobedient, deceived, enslaved to various lusts and pleasures, spending our life in malice and envy, hateful, hating one another. But when the kindness of God our Savior and His love for mankind appeared, He saved us, not on the basis of deeds which we have done in righteousness, but according to His mercy, by the washing of regeneration and renewing by the Holy Spirit.

TITUS 3:3-5

Harold Sala

What people think about you is not important. What God thinks about you is extremely important. The late Bob Cook used to say, "I give God the right to use people with whom I disagree." Which leads me to another important life lesson. I've learned to separate the cultural from the biblical. When I was coming up through the ranks, I began to realize there were individuals who disagreed with me. I believed my convictions were (and are) founded upon Scripture, but some of these issues are nonessentials, and they are not important enough to divide the world or to make enemies out of people who are your friends. That is one of the lessons I sometimes had to learn the hard way.

∞∞∞

Parting Thought

Life lessons are rarely fun. Sometimes they leave ugly scars. But how foolish to forget these experiences and waste the pain. Paul's admonishment in 1 Corinthians 10:11-12 is very instructive here:

> These things happened to them as an example, and they were written for our instruction, upon whom the ends of the ages have come. Therefore, let him who thinks he stands take heed that he does not fall.

Scars serve as reminders, but only if we choose to look at them. The same is true of the life lessons that have come our way. Let's choose to look, learn, and live.

5

A Bible Verse I Cling to More Than Ever

It was November 3, 1945. Twenty-six passengers were onboard the luxurious *Honolulu Clipper*. The giant flying boat featured a dining salon with world-class chefs, dressing rooms, lounges, sleeping berths, and even a private bridal suite in the rear of the aircraft.

Five and a half hours out of Honolulu, engine 3 began backfiring, shooting out flames. Then a second engine faltered, and the crew was forced to land the plane in the water about 650 miles east of Oahu. Hours later, a Navy escort carrier connected a towing line to the disabled flying boat and began tugging it back to port, the passengers now safely on the carrier. But after seven hours, the towrope broke. Another boat was brought along to attempt a new towline when a huge wave slammed it into the plane, causing damage so severe as to render it no longer worth the rescue. If left to bob on the waves, the *Clipper* would become a navigation hazard, so the decision was made to sink the plane.

Consider the high price of not hanging on. One of the most luxurious aircraft ever to fly was destroyed because a navy crew was unable to keep it connected to its rescue boat. What could possibly be more basic or—in this case—more disastrous?

Because of the damage of sin, you and I are rendered as powerless as that drifting airship. Left to ourselves, we bob up and down in the chilly waters around us. What we need, desperately, is a towline connecting us with our Rescuer, Jesus Christ.

In the kind provision of God, such a towline exists. It's nothing less sturdy than the Word of God itself. The thing is, that towline is a voluntary connection. God has made it available, but we have to make it personal by choosing to cling to His promises, His written Word.

As we are all on a different journey, we may cling to a different Bible verse. The Scriptures you are about to read are not necessarily claimed as life verses, but rather a towline to the faithfulness of God. As you read, I hope you grab a few of these for your own.

∽∾∽∾

Jill Briscoe

"Even when I am old and gray, O God, do not forsake me, until I declare Your strength to this generation, Your power to all who are to come" (Psalm 71:18).

This verse was written by David in his middle age. He was looking back on God's faithfulness, looking around at his own challenges at midlife, and also looking forward. David asked God for more years. That's where I am now. I am "old and gray." Sure, I could live another 10 or 20 years. Who knows? Spiritual gifts don't age, and my spiritual gift seems to involve kids—college kids. Amazingly, I'm still on college campuses and working with those kids because that's my spiritual gift.

I'm concerned about the millennials, and I know God has gifted me to be able to connect. So I have asked for more years to be able to do that.

Gail MacDonald

"We do not lose heart, but though our outer man is decaying, yet our inner man is being renewed day by day" (2 Corinthians 4:16).

I love the challenge that was given by Robertson McQuilkin regarding this verse. He said, "Outer beauty was given for young people, but inner beauty was given for people who are older." I take that very seriously. I can grow old gracefully knowing that this is what God meant to happen. The inner is what I'm supposed to pay attention to, not the outer.

Anne Graham Lotz

"'Rend your heart and not your garments.' Now return to the LORD your God, for He is gracious and compassionate, slow to anger, abounding in lovingkindness and relenting of evil" (Joel 2:13).

Even as judgment was coming on God's people, He said, in effect, "Even now if you'll rend your heart and not your garments, even now if you'll return to Me with all of your heart, who knows but that I might leave a blessing instead of bringing judgment!" That is my prayer for America right now. Even as judgment is coming, and I believe it's already begun, that we would rend our hearts. If God's people would repent of their sin, change their way of living, and return to God, He would bless us instead of judge us. That's my prayer.

Ravi Zacharias

"I am not ashamed of the gospel, for it is the power of God for salvation to everyone who believes, to the Jew first and also to the Greek" (Romans 1:16).

The power to transform a life is really the power God gives through His Word. Oftentimes you and I are nervous about sharing what we believe. It shows we are not at all certain about the power that lies within that verse. So the power to transform a life is really the power God gives through His Word.

Gary Chapman

"Fear thou not; for I am with thee: be not dismayed; for I am thy God: I will strengthen thee; yea, I will help thee; yea, I will uphold thee with the right hand of my righteousness" (Isaiah 41:10 KJV).

That's the old King James. I memorized it many years ago. Often in my journey, I go back to that verse. It's the awareness that God is with us that carries us through the hard times in life.

Michael Easley

"I love the LORD, because He hears my voice and my supplications. Because He has inclined His ear to me, therefore I shall call upon Him as long as I live" (Psalm 116:1-2).

If God never did one more thing for you or me, would we still love Him? At this stage of my life, the body is a lot older than the mind! I really do cling to Psalm 116. I think it's a marvelous song/poem of a man facing a lot of challenges, a lot of problems, yet he chose to begin with, "I love the Lord, because He hears my voice."

Dee Brestin

"As the bridegroom rejoices over the bride, so your God will rejoice over you" (Isaiah 62:5).

I think the only way we can turn from temptation is if we trust the love of God and believe He loves us just as this verse describes. As a woman I particularly identify with this metaphor that tells me I can trust Him.

Tony Evans

"I have been crucified with Christ; and it is no longer I who live, but Christ lives in me; and the life which I now live in the flesh I live by faith in the Son of God, who loved me and gave Himself up for me" (Galatians 2:20).

This verse serves as the basis for my true identity that I must continually go back to as I make decisions in my life.

June Hunt

"The Lord himself goes before you and will be with you; he will never leave you nor forsake you. Do not be afraid; do not be discouraged" (Deuteronomy 31:8 NIV).

I love this verse because so often we can feel alone. We can be in the middle of a crowd and still feel alone. We may feel that nobody understands our situation. And they may not, but the Lord Himself does.

Jan Silvious

"God hath not given us the spirit of fear; but of power, and of love, and of a sound mind" (2 Timothy 1:7 KJV).

As I grow older, I understand I am empowered by the Holy Spirit. I am empowered to do what I have to do. On days when I feel like saying, "I can't," the reality is I *can* because I have the Spirit within me. I have Christ within me. I can love even when it's sometimes difficult. Sometimes loving is not what it's cracked up to be. It's something you have to choose. I want to hang on to a sound mind and a mind that endures whatever I will walk through because that's God's gift. I don't have to bail out and say, "Oh, God, I'm overwhelmed. I can't take it." Instead, I should say, "God, You're still God. You're in control, and I will maintain a patient mind that endures." That's what I hang on to now.

Ron Hutchcraft

"Let the peace of Christ rule in your hearts, to which indeed you were called in one body; and be thankful" (Colossians 3:15).

To me, this verse establishes a fundamental decision-making principle. Try to get alone with Jesus when you have a decision to make. Other factors will come in and get you confused, but this verse says, "Let [allow, give permission to] the peace of Christ…" The word "rule" in the Greek means "be the umpire." What does the umpire do? He decides who is safe and who is out. That's what the peace of Christ is supposed to do: "This is the right choice." "That one is out for you. It's the wrong choice."

Erwin Lutzer

"If any of you lacks wisdom, let him ask of God, who gives to all generously and without reproach, and it will be given to him" (James 1:5).

The reason this verse is important to me is because as I go along in life, there are too many choices. Sometimes I've been counseling people on the telephone, and I need wisdom. I don't know how to navigate the situation. Or maybe it's a sermon I don't know how to put together, and it's Saturday afternoon. Then I cry to God for wisdom. There have been times when I've been sitting at my computer writing a book, and I honestly don't know what to say, and I say, "God, help me. This is Your moment!" Know what? God comes through!

Josh McDowell

"You will know the truth, and the truth will make you free" (John 8:32).

To my way of thinking, truth was not given to be merely cognitive. This is what separates me from most—not all, but most—apologists. I've never looked at truth for the sake of knowing truth. Truth, all truth in the Scriptures, was given to apply to relationships. Truth should always be personal. If your behavior, your family, your marriage (all your relationships) aren't based on truth lived out in those relationships, you're going to fail.

Art Rorheim

"None of these things move me, neither count I my life dear unto myself, so that I might finish my course with joy, and the ministry, which I have

received of the Lord Jesus, to testify the gospel of the grace of God" (Acts 20:24 *KJV*).

This verse expresses the heart of the apostle Paul. That makes it a verse that really grips my heart.

Stuart Briscoe

"Unto him that is able to do exceeding abundantly above all that we ask or think, according to the power that worketh in us, unto him be glory in the church by Christ Jesus throughout all ages, world without end. Amen" (Ephesians 3:20-21 *KJV*).

I think this passage is absolutely fundamental. The older you get, the more you realize what you don't know. You also realize all the things you haven't done. You are also aware of how minimal your impact has been on the world. You are accordingly reminded of your own fallenness and your own frailty. That will either push you into despair (you throw up your hands and say, "I quit") or you will say, "How desperately in need of divine unction I am!" Divine unction is all about what *He* is able to do according to the power that works within us.

Harold Sala

"Lo, I am with you always, even to the end of the age" (Matthew 28:20); *"Never will I leave you, never will I forsake you"* (Hebrews 13:5 *NIV*).

These two verses both express the reality that Christ is there, whether we feel it or not (and sometimes we don't). We don't operate on emotions, but the statements of Scripture. So I fall back on this: He will be there, no matter what the challenges, and no matter what we face. That is very clear.

Michael W. Smith

"How precious also are Your thoughts to me, O God! How vast is the sum of them! If I should count them, they would outnumber the sand. When I awake, I am still with You" (Psalm 139:17-18).

I go back to this passage all the time because even though I feel that I've grown up and I'm getting there, and I'm probably more mature now than I have ever been, I'm still on the journey, just as we all are. There are still those days when you become frazzled and lose perspective a little bit. You find yourself meandering down some crazy road, starting to feel unproductive. A thought pops into your head, *Man, I gotta get my act together.* Perhaps you're fighting this addiction or that addiction—whatever—and you start beating yourself up. That's when I say, "Wait a minute. I can't forget that His thoughts about me are precious. Those thoughts of His are vast, and there are so many good thoughts from Him they outnumber the grains of the sand." That reels me back every time. It gives me the right kind of perspective on how I should feel about myself.

Joni Eareckson Tada

"God demonstrates his own love for us in this: While we were still sinners, Christ died for us" (Romans 5:8 NIV).

So many of us Christians forget that the essence of God's love, His core plan, is to rescue sinners out of the kingdom of darkness. That means absolutely everything that happens to us—every suffering, every affliction, every hardship, every disappointment in life—is meant to challenge our man-made views about the love of God. I think that's why sitting in my wheelchair, I've come to see that affliction is what will drive us to the end of ourselves. Only then do we see the self-pity and the complaining, whining, discontent, peevish, and sour spirit we're made of. We're sinners in need of redemption! Let's keep the main thing the main thing.

∽∽∽

Parting Thought

A few years ago, my wife and I connected a pop-up camper to our minivan in order to take it to a service dealer. After driving several miles, we heard a metallic crunch and then felt a frightening bumping sensation. The trailer was slithering back and forth behind us—and into the bumper of our van! We thought it had been properly connected to the hitch, but it obviously wasn't. Thankfully, two chains (whose sole purpose is to keep the camper connected in emergencies like ours) kept us safe. They were our towlines! Without them, the untethered camper may have careened into oncoming traffic. We were able to slow down and get properly reconnected. Could it be that's what you and I need to do spiritually, right now? Get reconnected!

"I am the vine, you are the branches; he who abides in Me and I in him, he bears much fruit, for apart from Me you can do nothing" (John 15:5).

6

A Principle I'm Desperate to Pass On

He tried. He really did. But I was a lost cause—poor Dad.

Imagine being an intelligent man of science and yet unable to get your own child to grasp the fundamental principles of chemistry or physics. A gifted high school science teacher, not to mention pilot, photographer, and musician, my father transitioned to a career in electronic engineering. Yet he was simply unable to pass along his high school science principles to me. I never could grasp covalent bonds, atomic weights, or sidereal orbits. I honestly suspect my brain may have faulty wiring with these and a few other subjects.

Speaking of wiring, my wife and I once built an addition onto our house. Tight finances dictated we had to finish the interior ourselves (meaning...mostly Dad). As we bent electrical pipe for the wires, the teacher in Dad couldn't resist attempting to explain the basics of "supply" and "grounding" and "neutrals," and it all made sense at the time. But, honestly, I never really did get it.

I'm sure there are other things my dad tried to pass along to me that I failed to grasp. No doubt I drove the teacher in him absolutely crazy. (He's been kind enough to keep that to himself.)

But may I tell you one thing my dad *did*

manage to pass on? Tithing—giving money to the Lord's work. I watched the way Dad and Mom paid the bills every month. Church giving and other gifts were always first. And once that check was stuffed into the church envelope, it stayed on a small table, waiting for Sunday. You couldn't help but walk by and see it and know what was important to my parents. It wasn't that they were trying to show off. They were trying to show us kids something of extraordinary significance: the blessing of being a cheerful giver.

From the first paycheck my wife and I shared as newlyweds, we have likewise held an unwavering commitment to giving to the Lord's work. I would likely have had far less of a concept of biblical giving had it not been for two parents who were committed to handing this principle down to their children. And had my wife's parents not shown an equal commitment to biblical giving, there is no way she would be in agreement about the way we give.

It's a powerful example of one generation handing off the baton of faith to the next. But I wonder if I have been as intentional in transmitting this to our kids. A biblical sense of stewardship is just one of many values we should be passing on. But did I? Did we? Did our parenting convey a sense of holy desperation to impart other biblical principles? Only if you have moved into middle age can you appreciate the amount of brooding that goes on over these issues.

Let me ask you this directly. Have you ever thought through what you might place on a list titled "Principles I'm Desperate to Pass on to My Children"? It's a question we put to our contributors.

Tony Evans

I want to pass along the lesson that we must live all of life under God's rule. Don't assume you can pick and choose. Don't have God in one area and out of another. All of life must be under the rule of God. This is the truth I am desperate to pass on to my children and grandchildren.

Jan Silvious

Philippians 4:6-7 tells us, "Be anxious for nothing, but in everything by prayer and supplication with thanksgiving"—primarily with thanksgiving—"let your requests be made known to God. And the peace of God, which surpasses all comprehension, will guard your hearts and your minds in Christ Jesus." That is a truth that sustains me, and I believe it will sustain my children and grandchildren in these days that are filled with anxiety, when there seems to be nothing to hang on to. But we don't have to be anxious because God is on the throne. Jesus has finished it all, taken care of it, and we can come to Him with thanksgiving, thanksgiving that He's there! Thanksgiving that He has it under control! We can tell Him what the need is, and then we will have peace in the midst of the roughest storm.

Steve Brown

The older you get, the more you see what's important and what isn't. It's not the last book that I wrote; it's my daughter. It's not how many broadcasts I've done. It's not how much money I made or what kind of house I lived in. It's our grandchildren. The one thing I want them to get—and they do (I'm overwhelmed and so glad): "Jesus loves me this I know, for the Bible tells me so." If you get that, everything else is small stuff.

Dee Brestin

I want to pass on the importance of praying the Psalms. I learned from Dietrich Bonhoeffer that it's a common error among believers to think the soul can pray by itself. In order to pray with real efficacy and strength, we need God's prayer book. We need the Psalms, and that has radically changed my prayer life. I'm teaching my children and grandchildren how to pray the Psalms.

Jill Briscoe

Don't waste the pain. Let it drive you deeper to God, and use the pain that comes into your life as a place of blessing for others. Learn to maximize the good times instead of just coasting. Learn to handle success, which is far harder than handling failure and pain.

Point to Ponder

We will not conceal them from their children,
but tell to the generation to come the praises of the LORD,
and His strength and His wondrous works that He has done.
PSALM 78:4

Gary Chapman

I would pass on to my children, my grandchildren, and my great-grandchildren the reality that Jesus Christ is Lord. He invaded human history so we could know Him in a personal way. That's fundamental. Once they understand that and accept it and receive Christ as their salvation, I think the thing I would next impress upon them is that each of us is uniquely gifted by God. God wants to use what He's given to us to further His purposes in the world. Life's greatest meaning is found in taking what God has given you and developing it and then using it to interface and interact with other people. That's really what I would hope they would experience in their lives.

Walter Wangerin

I doubt there's just a single truth I would want to pass on. On the other hand, I hope I *am* a truth to my children and grandchildren, particularly in these portions of my life where I have come to wisdom. When I got cancer and was lying down all the time, one of my grandchildren, Emma, went to my wife and said, "Would it hurt him if I lie down beside him?" Such tender sympathy and such care. I hope that in that moment I communicated the truth to her in my reception.

Anne Graham Lotz

God speaks through the Word. There is a living God. He is in heaven, but He speaks personally through the Scriptures. You can hear His voice if you open up the ears of your heart to listen as you read. You can hear Him speak and then you can talk to Him in prayer. When you talk to Him, He hears you. He's a prayer-hearing, prayer-answering, miracle-working God. I believe my three children have grasped that and so have my grandchildren. That's something I want to pass on to the next generation.

POINT TO PONDER

All Scripture is inspired by God and profitable for teaching,
for reproof, for correction, for training in righteousness;
so that the man of God may be adequate,
equipped for every good work.

2 TIMOTHY 3:16-17

George Verwer

Salvation is by grace through trusting and believing in Jesus. You may still have some things wrong in your life, and you may not have your theology totally correct, but if you trust Jesus as your Savior, I'll see you in heaven! I hope I've already passed that on to my children and grandchildren—it's all about Jesus. That is the message of grace. When they fail and when they sin (as their father and grandfather have), "He is faithful and righteous to forgive us our sins and to cleanse us from all unrighteousness" (1 John 1:9).

Ron Hutchcraft

It's all about Jesus. I want my kids and grandkids truly to know that when you sin, you're not just breaking rules, you are breaking Jesus's heart. When you put money in the offering, you are not giving it to the church or the organization or the pastor. You are—like the little boy did with his lunch—putting it in the hands of Jesus. Giving an offering is all about Jesus. The message we have to share with people is not about family values or politics or lifestyle. It is all about Jesus. "I determined," the apostle said, "to know nothing among you except Jesus Christ, and Him crucified" (1 Corinthians 2:2). This is all I want them to know. It's Jesus. It's *just* Jesus. It's *all* about Jesus.

Erwin Lutzer

A truth I'm desperate to pass on could be summed up in just one sentence: "The enjoyment of God is better than all other achievements or successes in the world." Whenever I'm asked to give an autograph somewhere, I always include Psalm 16:11, which says, "In thy presence is fulness of joy; at thy right hand there are pleasures for evermore" (KJV). If only we could remember that God and His ways are best.

James MacDonald

What I want to tell our kids and grandkids is to be patient. God isn't finished with you yet. This isn't a sprint. If you've had a bad day, a bad week, a bad month, or a bad quarter, all is not lost. God's grace continues to cover those areas in our lives that need to improve, need to change. His mercies are new every morning.

POINT TO PONDER

He has said to me, "My grace is sufficient for you,
for power is perfected in weakness." Most gladly, therefore,
I will rather boast about my weaknesses,
so that the power of Christ may dwell in me.

2 CORINTHIANS 12:9

Josh McDowell

I've always desired to equip my children to stand out from the culture, because if you're not willing to be different, you will never, ever be a true follower of Jesus and impact your world. Given the influence of the Internet, pornography, and so much secularization of the faith, I have more of a responsibility than ever to impact my children and grandchildren. But here's the thing. If you're not purposeful, you will have many regrets when you get older. Me, I want my children and grandchildren to know how to stand tall in a depraved world.

Bob Moeller

One truth I want to leave with my children and grandchildren is from the book of Proverbs: "A good name is more desirable than great riches" (Proverbs 22:1 NIV). You can lose your money and get it back. You can get sick and regain your health. You can be fired from your job and find another one. But you seem to get only one reputation in life. So it is critically important to guard that carefully. We need to build and keep a reputation for being godly and filled with integrity. Who you are when people are watching must be who you are when they are not. This is something you never want to compromise or trade away for any short-term gain from an impulsive choice at the moment. Your reputation—who you really are—needs to honor God.

Art Rorheim

What would I hope to pass on to my kids and grandkids? That they would truly be God's witnesses and not be ashamed. I'd like for them to live out 1 Corinthians 15:58, that they would be "stedfast, unmoveable, always abounding in the work of the Lord" (KJV). What I'm happy about right now is the fact that my grandchildren and great-grandchildren—all of them—know the Lord as their Savior. I hope they will not be satisfied just to be saved, but they will be on fire spiritually, really excited about following the Lord wherever He leads them. That's the heartbeat I'd like to see in all my grandkids—that they would carry the Message with enthusiasm.

POINT TO PONDER

How then will they call on Him
in whom they have not believed?
How will they believe in Him whom they have not heard?
And how will they hear without a preacher?
ROMANS 10:14

Ravi Zacharias

Every day matters. I think that so often what happens is we wait for landmark moments, defining decisions. *Where am I going to go to school? How am I going to take care of my health? Which doctor am I going to see? What job am I going to take? Whom am I going to date? Whom am I going to marry?* All of these things are critical decisions, but the fact of the matter is, every day counts and is important. The hymn writer writes, "Day by Day," then somebody else writes, "I Need Thee Every Hour" and someone else comes along and says, "Moment by Moment." Jesus tells us to pray, "Give us this day." And that daily bread, I think, can go way beyond just what we need for spiritual sustenance. The choices we make have an impact on all of these things. So I would say to my children and grandchildren: Every day matters.

Harold Sala

The Bible is a changeless book in a changing world. I think it's extremely important that we not trivialize the Bible or reject it because our culture has changed. Basically, we're living in a pagan culture. One of the things I live for now is to see my grandkids, all eight of them, grounded in the Word and committed to the same principles I am committed to, and making their lives count for the Lord. We have no guarantees, but thank God we're seeing this take place. I hope I live long enough to see a number of my grandchildren going into Christian work or doing medical work on the mission field. I want to pass the baton to them.

Michael W. Smith

I would say two things to my kids and grandkids: What's the number one command? "Love the Lord your God with all your heart, and with all your soul, and with all your mind, and with all your strength" (Mark 12:30). That would be the number one thing. Then number two is, "Love your neighbor as yourself" (Mark 12:31). I think we find one of the hardest commands, one of the most challenging verses in all of Scripture, in Philippians 2:3, "Regard one another as more important than yourselves." That's a tall order, but I think it's doable. If you really are rooted and grounded and have embraced grace and know that you're absolutely loved, you can approach all your peers, colleagues, and friends and consider their needs more than you do your own.

Parting Thought

He started out with high hopes and even higher ambitions. The eldest son of an English banker, John was headed for a career in the British Parliament. But when his father went bankrupt, John pursued the ministry, becoming the first Anglican bishop of Liverpool. Many have read his books, *Holiness* or *A Call to Prayer*, but few are aware that J.C. Ryle experienced great personal loss.

Just two years after marrying his sweetheart, Matilda Louisa, Ryle lost her to influenza after she gave birth to their daughter. Ryle married a second time to Jessie Walker, but she died at the age of 38, having been sickly all but six months of their 11-year marriage. His third wife, Henrietta, lived longer than the first two, but she died more than a decade before her husband.

In spite of his personal pain (imagine burying three wives), J.C. Ryle was unshakable in his faith, and determined to pass along that faith to his children. Although some of the family details are lost to history, we know that Ryle's son, Edward, also a clergyman, became Bishop of Exeter, Bishop of Winchester, and finally, Dean of Westminster. When he died, he was buried in a spot close to the tomb of the Unknown Warrior. Dean Ryle Street in Westminster, named in his honor, stands as a permanent tribute to his worthy life. Clearly, J.C. Ryle handed off the baton of faith to his children, and that is why his words now close this chapter:

"He that has trained his children for heaven, rather than for earth— for God, rather than for man—he is the parent that will be called wise at last."

7

A Favorite Quotation of Mine

Cultural crazes. America has never lacked for them. From the Rubik's Cube of the 1980s, Super Soakers from the 1990s, and Razor Scooters from the 2000s, we've always had cultural obsessions. One of our current cultural crazes is our extreme fascination with quotations and inspirational posters. Pinterest has likely fueled this fascination into a movement of its own. A sizable percentage of Pinterest's traffic is associated with quotations.

I confess to being a quotation collector. I have a file on my computer called "E-quotes." Its entries number in the hundreds. If that isn't obsession enough, I also keep a blank paper journal that allows me to glue in photocopies of quips or handwritten quotations. May I share a few of my favorites?

> Millions of hells of sinners cannot come near to exhaust infinite grace.
>
> ~Samuel Rutherford

> It is possible to be religiously active and spiritually corrupt.
>
> ~Robert A. Cook

Heal me of this lust of mine to always vindicate myself.

~Augustine

If sinners will be damned, at least let them leap to hell over our bodies. And if they will perish, let them perish with our arms around their knees, imploring them to stay. If hell must be filled, at least let it be filled in the teeth of our exertions, and let not one go there unwarned and unprayed for.

~Charles Haddon Spurgeon

I'm guessing you like quotations too. So, it turns out, did the slate of contributors we interviewed. But, sometimes, just as important as the quotations themselves, are the stories behind the quotations.

Nancy DeMoss Wolgemuth

I'm a big collector of quotations. In fact, on Twitter, I mostly quote old dead guys. I live a lot in those quotations. But I have one that's especially meaningful to me. It's on a small marble paperweight that my dad had on his desk. It was given to me after he went to be with the Lord. It's just a couplet. I don't even know who originally said it, but it's familiar to many of us. It was so important to my dad, and it's become something of a mantra to me:

> Only one life— 'twill soon be past;
> Only what's done for Christ will last.

Michael Easley

I was at Dallas Seminary when Vance Havner (in his eighties at the time) was preaching in chapel. Here was this frail man wearing big trifocals. When he got up, you could see those huge eyes of his. His message was magnificent. At the end of it he walked away from the pulpit but then shuffled back. Understand that back then Dallas Seminary was mostly a school of men. Dr. Havner said, "Gentlemen, I just feel compelled to ask you to pray for me. I've never done this before, but would you pray that I don't die a fool?" He could barely walk. He shuffled. I was sitting with two buddies, and we knew exactly what he meant. Leaving that chapel, my thought was, *Is there any hope for any of us? This guy's so frail, physically, and yet he's asking that he not die a fool.* I thought, *Wow, that's transparent. That's real. That's vulnerable.* More than 30 years later, I still remember the moment.

Anne Graham Lotz

I have a little plaque in the bathroom where I do my makeup that my mother, Ruth, gave me. It was the plaque that was by her mirror when she was growing up in China. It's a verse from Titus: "Looking for that blessed hope, and the glorious appearing of the great God and our Saviour Jesus Christ" (Titus 2:13 KJV). That was precious to my mother, and it's very precious to me. I'm looking for the blessed hope and the glorious appearing of our Lord Jesus Christ. I'm looking for that more today than I did yesterday!

Stuart Briscoe

Albert Einstein is said to have kept this quotation on his desk at Princeton: "Not everything that can be counted counts. Not everything that counts can be counted." This has become a favorite of mine.

POINT TO PONDER

We fix our eyes not on what is seen, but on what is unseen, since what is seen is temporary, but what is unseen is eternal.
2 CORINTHIANS 4:18 (NIV)

Dee Brestin

C.S. Lewis said of Jesus, "He's not a great teacher. He didn't give us that option. He is either a liar, a lunatic, or the Son of God." That is what we have to decide.

Tony Evans

Corrie ten Boom said, "There is no pit so deep that He is not deeper still." When ministry seems overwhelming, this quote gives me comfort that God will meet me at my lowest point. There was a time when it looked as if the church would not be able to pay its bills, and I had to hold on to that truth.

Steve Brown

Billy Sunday said, "A sinner can repent, but stupid is forever." That's a favorite quotation, and I have *piles* of quotations. I'm Reformed and a Calvinist, but I like Luther. When somebody asked Luther about works of penance he said, "What is it about our arrogance that makes us think that anything we could ever do is more sufficient than the blood of Jesus Christ?"

Michael Card

One of my favorites is from Brennan Manning. He said, "You don't have to be good for God to love you. God loves you so you *can* be good."

POINT TO PONDER

God, being rich in mercy, because of His great love
with which He loved us, even when we were dead in
our transgressions, made us alive together with Christ
(by grace you have been saved).
EPHESIANS 2:4-5

Gail MacDonald

My journey in prayer has basically been modeled after George Mueller, who said, "Learn to move people by prayer alone." That quotation can get you a long way when you think you have to help God answer prayer. This has become a catalyst resulting in a total metamorphosis in my life. For the past ten years, I have watched God do miracles without my helping Him. We all need to learn to move people by prayer alone!

Ron Hutchcraft

"I have no greater joy than this, to hear of my children walking in the truth" (3 John 4). For a recent birthday, my children gave me a plaque that includes this verse. I choked up because this verse represents a legacy, the greatest desire of any parent. That verse really refreshes my heart.

James MacDonald

William Carey said, "Expect great things from God. Attempt great things for God." Another quote I like is from Oswald Chambers: "I have never met the man I could despair of after discerning what lies in me apart from the grace of God."

Josh McDowell

"There's nothing too great in my life for God's power to deal with, nor anything too insignificant for His love to be concerned with." Until you realize this, you are not truly free. You are not truly free when you believe God can deal with the great things in your life. You are truly free when you realize He can also deal with the little things in your life.

Bob Moeller

"If you keep your vows in life, they will keep you." I've seen this truth play out over and over again, particularly in marriage. If you keep the vows you promised, as life goes on, you will see how they bring to you all the goodness, all the blessings, all the fulfillment, all the fruit that anybody could wish for. I've never ever regretted the vows I've made, particularly in marriage. By honoring and by keeping those vows, I've seen innumerable blessings come from them. So if you keep your vows, in the end they will keep you.

Art Rorheim

I noticed on Jerry Falwell's tomb this quotation: "You can tell much about the character of a person by how much it takes for him to get discouraged." We know that discouragement is the devil's greatest tool. So many people fail, and they throw in the towel with regard to serving the Lord because they have failed. We all become discouraged, but we get up and press on. If we've failed, we just need to ask the Lord to forgive us and press on. Another favorite quotation of mine is from Hunter S. Thompson: "Life should not be a journey to the grave with the intention of arriving safely in a pretty and well-preserved body, but rather to skid in broadside...thoroughly used up, totally worn out, and loudly proclaiming, 'Wow! What a ride!'"

POINT TO PONDER

Have I not commanded you? Be strong and courageous!
Do not tremble or be dismayed,
for the LORD your God is with you wherever you go.
JOSHUA 1:9

Colin Smith

Robert Murray M'Cheyne said, "My people's greatest need is my personal holiness." It's a marvelous phrase that affects the way I minister. As a pastor, I ask, "What is the greatest need of my people? What do they most need? My preaching? My leadership? My vision? My presence?" No! M'Cheyne said, "My people's greatest need is my personal holiness." That's a life lesson for me, and I have really valued it.

Michael W. Smith

St. Francis of Assisi is credited with this favorite: "Preach the gospel at all times, and when necessary use words." That's still one of my favorites. I also have a Bob Goff quotation on a Post-it Note on my bathroom mirror that says, "Love God, love people, and do stuff." Just change the world. Go do stuff. Go make a contribution every day. Just do stuff for people. I love that!

Joe Stowell

"Our lives are not made by the dreams we dream but by the choices that we make." I think that is pivotal for us. Obviously, we come into life with dreams: the dreams of what might be, dreams of what our marriage will be like, dreams of our children. We're full of dreams. But those dreams are often destroyed by making the wrong choices. For example, standing at the altar with my beautiful bride, I might dream of a wonderful life together, but then I choose to be selfish, choose to be unkind, choose to be unforgiving. Suddenly, that dream just crumbles before me. At the heart of my life and yours are the choices we make. My life today is the sum total of all the choices I've ever made.

George Verwer

"Where two or three of the Lord's people are gathered together, sooner or later there's a mess." I wrote this proverb. To summarize, it means that God, in His grace and His mercy, because of Calvary, can do phenomenal things even in messy situations. God is working. He's working in the world. God is doing more things in our country in these messy days than most people realize. When people embrace this kind of thinking they are happier, they are more fulfilled, they are bigger hearted, they are grace awakened. It's absolutely transformational.

> Who is a God like You, who pardons iniquity and
> passes over the rebellious act of the remnant of His possession?
> He does not retain His anger forever,
> because He delights in unchanging love.
>
> MICAH 7:18

Jill Briscoe

"Keep calm and carry on." Unlike most people who refer to this quotation, I know where it came from. I was a child in Liverpool when we were bombed by the Nazis. At the age of six, I heard Churchill's famous speech on the radio: "They're coming!" We were told, "Pack your suitcase if you live on the coast" (which we did) "and when the church bells ring"—which was the sign of the invasion—"run!" My mother went to pack my little suitcase. An hour after his famous speech, Churchill came back to give instructions to England. The first thing he did was to call the entire country to prayer the next day. Imagine all England kneeling and praying: men, women, children in the streets and, of course, in the churches—they did! Then the next thing Churchill said was, "Keep calm and carry on." Leaflets and posters had been made bearing this message. They were stashed in all the churches. We were told that when the Germans approached, we were to get those posters and slap them on trees and every public place so that when the Nazis arrived, they would see that this was the British! We would fight on the beaches, we would do all that. It's a moving story to me because I was there as a little child. The slogan reminds me of my lifelong struggle with worry.

Joni Eareckson Tada

I have a favorite poem. It was written by a woman named Madame Lyons, a French noblewoman thrown into a dungeon on charges trumped up by jealous church officials. For ten long years she was in that stinking dungeon, and there she wrote beautiful hymns and beautiful poetry. I memorized one of her poems shortly after I got out of the hospital and was getting used to living life in a wheelchair. She wrote:

> *A little bird I am,*
> *Shut from the fields of air;*
> *And in my cage I sit and sing*
> *To Him who placed me there;*
> *Well pleased a prisoner to be*
> *Because, my God, it pleases Thee.*
> *Naught have I else to do;*
> *I sing the whole day long;*
> *And He whom most I love to please,*
> *Doth listen to my song:*
> *He caught and He bound my wandering wing,*
> *But still He bends to hear me sing.*
> *My cage confines me round;*
> *Abroad I cannot fly;*
> *But though my wing is closely bound,*
> *My heart's at liberty;*
> *My prison walls cannot control*
> *The flight, the freedom of the soul.*

Oh! It is good to soar
These bolts and bars above,
To Him whose purpose I adore,
Whose providence I love;
And in His mighty will to find
The joy, the freedom, of the mind.

Ravi Zacharias

If I had to choose just one quotation, I think I would hark back to my conversion and the following verse of Charles Wesley:

Long my imprisoned spirit lay
Fast bound in sin and nature's night;
Thine eye diffused a quickening ray—
I woke, the dungeon flamed with light;
My chains fell off, my heart was free,
I rose, went forth, and followed Thee.

I love these words intertwining the sovereignty of God and the responsibility of the individual, and how God in that inward "I" quickens you and then awakens your will to follow Him. I would say that stanza of his hymn "And Can It Be That I Should Gain" is one of my favorite passages of all time.

Parting Thought

S.D. Gordon, who lived in the late nineteenth and early twentieth centuries, wrote a series of bestselling books titled *Quiet Thoughts*. In his treatise on prayer, he makes this observation—a fitting conclusion to a chapter full of great quotations:

> The great people of the earth today are the people who pray. I do not mean those who talk about prayer, nor those who say they believe in prayer, nor yet those who can explain about prayer; but I mean these people who take time and pray. They have not time. It must be taken from something else. This something else is important, very important, and pressing, but still less important and less pressing than prayer. There are people who put prayer first, and group the other items in life's schedule around and after prayer. Prayer is man giving God a footing on the contested territory of this earth. The man in full touch of purpose with God praying, insistently praying—that man is God's footing on the enemy's soil. And the Holy Spirit within that man, on the new spot, will insist on the enemy's retreat in Jesus the Victor's name. That is prayer. Shall we not, every one of us, increase God's footing down upon His prodigal earth!

8

What I Want on My Tombstone

A walk through a cemetery is a trek through dichotomy. The lawn is perfect, the bushes are trimmed, and the view is all serenity. Yet the landscape of a grieving soul is a barren desert. Instead of serenity, there is an intense sobriety.

But beyond sobriety, cemeteries offer intrigue carved in granite impossible to find elsewhere. Unlike today's minimalist epitaphs (mainly name and date of the deceased's birth and death)—history offers many examples of epitaphs that range from confessional to comedic. Here are a few of my favorites:

> Here lies an honest lawyer—that is Strange.
> Sir John Strange (1696–1754)

From a cemetery at Bristol, England's Bath Abbey:

> Here lies Ann Mann.
> She lived an old maid and she died an old Mann.

In Woolwich Churchyard:

> As I am now, so you must be.
> Therefore prepare to follow me.

Added by his widow:

> To follow you, I'm not content
> Unless I know which way you went

From a churchyard near London:

> Stop, reader! I have left a world
> In which there was a world to do;
> Fretting and stewing to be rich—
> Just such a fool as you

Consider the prodigious progeny of William Stratton, who lived in central London:

> Here lies the body of
> William Stratton of Paddington,
> Buried 18th day of May, 1734, aged 97 years;
> who had by his first wife 28 children;
> by his second 17; was own father to 45;
> grandfather to 86; great-grandfather to 23.
> In all 154 children.

For nearly 50 years, Henry Clemitshaw served as church organist for the Wakefield Parish church. His epitaph reads in part:

> Now like an organ, robb'd of pipes and breath,
> Its keys and stops are useless made by death.
> Tho' mute and motionless in ruins laid,
> Yet when rebuilt by more than mortal aid,
> This instrument, new voiced, and tuned, shall raise

To God, its builder, hymns of endless praise

From Lydford churchyard, Dartmoor (southwest England):

Here lies, in horizontal position,
the outside case of George Routleigh, Watchmaker;
whose abilities in that line were
an honor to his profession.
Integrity was the Mainspring,
and prudence the Regulator,
of all the actions of his life.
Humane, generous, and liberal,
his Hand never stopped till he had relieved distress...
He had the art of disposing his time so well,
that his hours glided away in
one continual round of pleasure and delight,
until an unlucky minute put a period to his existence.
He departed this life November 14, 1802, aged 57,
wound up in hopes of being taken in hand by his Maker;
and of being thoroughly cleaned, repaired,
and set a-going in the world to come.
George Routleigh, Watchmaker

It's one thing to ponder, or perhaps chuckle, at epitaphs collected in a book (I own two such anthologies). Yet it's quite a bit more sobering to process your own epitaph. What do you want carved on your tombstone? Have you ever given it a thought? Here is what people told me.

Steve Brown

Born 1940-Died...A lot happened in that hyphen!

Tony Evans

He knew God and helped others to know Him too.

Michael Card

That is a topic I typically don't think about, but if I had to choose something, it might be "Slave of Christ" or something like that—modeled after my grandfather, a guy I admired.

Dee Brestin

I already have my tombstone because I will be next to my husband, and it says, "For me to live is Christ and to die is gain." Our lives are so full because of Christ, and yet the best is yet to come.

Josh McDowell

"He followed Jesus, loved his wife, and spent time with his children." To me, if you go through life and accomplish many "great things" for the kingdom but lose your marriage and family, you have failed. If you are a true follower of Christ, you will love your wife. You will also love and spend time with your children.

POINT TO PONDER

Each individual among you also is to
love his own wife even as himself,
and the wife must see to it that she respects her husband.

EPHESIANS 5:33

Erwin Lutzer

"He loved the gospel" is what I'd like to have on my tombstone. If I could have that, I would die satisfied. There are many messages out there. There are many speakers on exciting topics, but what we really need is a Savior to save us from our sins. There's a second option I wouldn't mind for my tombstone. I'm not sure I'm worthy of this, so I'm just putting out the idea: "He walked with God." Think, for example, of Enoch, who walked with God (Genesis 5:24). If you could have *that* on your tombstone, you would die very satisfied, and I believe Jesus would probably say, "Well done!"

Jan Silvious

"She loved well and she tried to reach us." I would like to think that after I'm gone, the love I have extended toward family, friends, and others will be recognized for what it was. Because sometimes love doesn't come in packages we identify as love. But I would hope that everyone in my life would know I tried to show them love even though it may not have been in a way that they understood at the time.

Gary Chapman

Years ago, I went to a cemetery and found the grave of a lady named Lottie Moon who served as a missionary in China. Southern Baptists named their annual missions offering the "Lottie Moon Christmas offering." As children, we all learned about Lottie Moon and her ministry. I was eager to find her tombstone. So I searched among the graves until I found it. To be frank, I was a little surprised to find that it was a small stone. On the stone I read these simple words—"Faithful Unto Death." Right there, I wept. I said, "God, that's what I want—to be faithful unto death." If those words can be truly said of me, I will be happy.

Nancy DeMoss Wolgemuth

I think the one phrase I would want on my tombstone might be this: "Handmaiden of the Lord" or "Bondservant of the Lord." They both mean the same thing. In Luke 1, an angel tells Mary that her life is about to be upended and turned upside down and inside out—that God has a plan and a purpose for her life that is humanly impossible. I love Mary's response. She says in verse 38, "I am the Lord's servant...May your word to me be fulfilled." I love that verse. I'd like to think that my life had been lived as the servant, the handmaiden of the Lord, and that whatever He wanted me to do, whatever He assigned to me, I said, "Yes, Lord."

Michael Easley

Vance Havner, I think, said it best. You really can't improve on this statement: "Just a preacher." I think at the end of the day we're just tools, we're just servants. We're just hands and feet to the gospel. I'd like to be able to look back and feel I was used of God and to know I was faithful to the task.

POINT TO PONDER

You shall follow the LORD your God and fear Him;
and you shall keep His commandments, listen to His voice,
serve Him, and cling to Him.
DEUTERONOMY 13:4

George Verwer

"Be ye stedfast, unmoveable, always abounding in the work of the Lord, forasmuch as ye know that your labour is not in vain in the Lord" (1 Corinthians 15:58 KJV). That's probably too long for a tombstone, so maybe just the words "Keep goin'."

Ravi Zacharias

It's funny. Just recently over lunch this became the topic of conversation with a gentleman who was talking about this question. What I would definitely want on my tombstone is what I saw on my grandmother's gravestone and put on my mother's: "Because I live, you will live also" (John 14:19). I would put a postscript beneath that: "I little understood the depth and breadth of what life actually meant until I found Him."

Anne Graham Lotz

"Just give me Jesus." I'm expecting any moment that I'm going to hear the trumpet sound, and I'm going to be caught up in the air to be with Jesus. So I'm not sure I'm going to have a tombstone. But if so, I would want to have a Scripture verse on it. But I also love the phrase, "Just give me Jesus." It really sums up my goal in life.

Ron Hutchcraft

My dad's tombstone just says, "Husband, Father." That would be a good statement, I think. I love David's "tombstone," if you could put it that way. Acts 13:36 says, "David, after he had served the purpose of God in his own generation, fell asleep." That's a pretty good tombstone for anybody: "I did what He created me for." I'm not sure I would begin to merit that. "He served the Lord's purpose in his generation"—is there any better reason for life?

James MacDonald

"Your words were found and I ate them, and Your words became for me a joy and the delight of my heart; for I have been called by Your name, O LORD God of hosts" (Jeremiah 15:16). The great passion of my life has been putting God's Word in front of people in a way that causes them to be passionate about it, to experience it personally. I was an 18- or 19-year-old kid, and I had already been following Christ, but I never had been deeply into God's Word. So when God's Word took hold of me, God took hold of me. My joy and deep longing has been to see other people have that experience too.

Bob Moeller

I've already thought about my tombstone. I think what I would like to have said is, "He loved the Lord his God with all his heart soul, mind, and strength, and he loved his neighbor as himself." The reason that would be important is Jesus said those were the two greatest commandments in life. Nothing we could attempt to do or be would surpass that. He commanded us to love God with all of our heart and to love each other in the same way. No force in this fallen world or in the wicked kingdom of our adversary can defeat love. I feel I've fallen way short of that, but if I could live my life the way that I truly would want to, people would look at my tombstone and say, "Yeah, that's true."

POINT TO PONDER

Be very careful to observe the commandment and the law which Moses the servant of the LORD commanded you, to love the LORD your God and walk in all His ways and keep His commandments and hold fast to Him and serve Him with all your heart and with all your soul.

JOSHUA 22:5

Harold Sala

I am reminded of the guy who asked his friend, "When you are in your casket and your friends are standing there, what do you want them to say?" His friend replied: "Look! He's moving!" For 15 years I hosted a television program, and I would ask my guests, "How would you like to be remembered?" The responses were interesting. Ironically, I have not given this question enough thought. I suppose this inscription would be good: "Here lies a man who believed God, and God honored his belief."

Colin Smith

I once preached on the biblical character of Simeon and addressed this exact question, "What do you want on your tombstone?" Simeon's life can be summarized as follows: "He was upright and devout. He sought after Christ, and the Holy Spirit rested upon him." If that could be said of me on my tombstone, I would be so very grateful.

Joni Eareckson Tada

I've often thought about what I want on my tombstone. When I was little, just growing up, when it was time for the family to go to bed and the lights would be turned out, we would hear—called from around the house—"See you in the morning! See you in the morning!" I would say that to my sisters as I went off to sleep, "See you in the morning." I think I might like that on my tombstone: "I'll see you in the morning."

Parting Thought

Guy de Maupassant was a Frenchman with a talent for writing and a penchant for women. His short story, "The Necklace," tells of a greedy young woman with an insatiable thirst for the good life.

Ironically, her life and that of the man who loves her are both destroyed by her unchecked passions.

Paradoxically, in real life, Maupassant was himself a troubled soul, desperate for solitude and obsessed with a sense of self-preservation. He had a psychotic fear of persecution and death, perhaps the result of syphilis. After an unsuccessful attempt to take his own life, he was committed to a private asylum in Paris where he soon died, but not before preparing his own epitaph: "I have coveted everything and taken pleasure in nothing."

Now, contrast that darksome life with that of Samuel Rabanks, steward of England's Earl of Danby. It's unlikely you have ever heard of Mr. Rabanks, a believer who lived and died in the 1600s. Yet, his tombstone speaks with an eloquence that is its own sermon:

> His life was an academy of virtue,
> His conversation a precedent for piety,
> His estate a storehouse for charity,
> His good name a place for innocency,
> His death a passage to eternity,
> His eternity a perfection of glory;
> Where he now sits, triumphs and sings with the angels,
> Archangels and cherubim and seraphim;
> Holy, holy, holy
> To him that is, and that was, and that is to come.
> Here is a life worth living—
> and a home going worth celebrating!

9

A Regret That Still Haunts Me

If regret had a poster child, Maud Muller would be the face. Born into poverty, she lived a quiet life on a quiet farm just outside the city. Her house was unremarkable, her wardrobe shabby, and her prospects dim. Still, like most young girls, Maud hungered deep inside for something more. That something was a someone, a judge from the city.

He sauntered onto Maud's farm one afternoon, greeting her from his horse and requesting a cool glass of water. She cheerfully obliged him, thirsty herself—for conversation. Maud's bare feet and tattered dress made it awkward for the two of them. She was as aware of her own poverty as she was of the judge's wealth.

Yet the more they talked, the more comfortable each became. Maud was lovely. But still better, she was kind and honest and hardworking. The couple talked and laughed, sharing that quiet sense of knowing born of attraction. Then the judge expressed his thanks and turned down the road back to the city.

With every step of the judge's horse, Maud sighed and dreamed. More than anything, she wished this man could be her husband. She saw herself married, in love, her parents cared for, and herself feeding the hungry and clothing the poor. If only Maud had taken just a bit more initiative with him...

More than anything, the judge wanted Maud for his wife. He saw himself enveloped in her loving and quiet words, enjoying her singing and sweet smile. The judge briefly dreamed of trading his considerable wealth to buy the better gold of purity and kindness that was Maud. If only he had taken just a bit more initiative with her...

Back home, reclined in luxury, a sense of propriety stole the luster from the judge's dream. His proud mother and sisters could never stoop to such a low marriage. Hadn't he best aim higher?

So he did. He married a woman whose dowry and standing in high society was deemed suitable. As for Maud, she eventually wed a poor, uneducated man and had many children. Both of them regretted their choices, thinking often of that golden afternoon now gone.

John Greenleaf Whittier's haunting story of Maud Muller ends with an immortal couplet:

> *Of all sad words*
> *Of tongue or pen,*
> *The saddest are these:*
> *"It might have been."*

Not an honest soul among us lives without it-might-have-been moments. Some of us have our pockets jammed with them. For others, a memory is tucked away just far enough to almost forget, but not quite. What do the authors and preachers and musicians you know regret? Let's find out.

If I Could Do It All Over Again

Art Rorheim

My biggest regrets are people I didn't witness to. I missed an amazing opportunity when I met one of my heroes from the Chicago Cubs, Andy Pafko. He was an All-Star player, and I once had the opportunity to play golf with him. He rode in my cart for 18 holes. Being with that amazing man, I had so many questions for him and wanted to hear what his life was all about. Then I realized I hadn't witnessed to him, and right after that he left. I was under such conviction. I said, "I'm going to call him and see if I can spend some more time with him." So I called him, and he said, "Well, I'm busy right now, but maybe in a couple of months we can get together again." The next thing I heard, he had passed away. To me, that was a real regret. I should have witnessed to Andy, but I was so interested in what I wanted to get from him I didn't represent God very well.

Jill Briscoe

When Stuart and I left England to move to America, we left behind two widowed mothers. I knew my mom would never come (and she didn't). That was the hardest thing I ever did, telling her we were going to America and taking her three grandchildren away. Obviously, we couldn't afford to run back and forth across the Atlantic. Yet I could have written Mom more. I could have borrowed money and gone. I could have done more. But I just have to let God deal with that. If past hurts are not put at the cross and blessed by the Spirit, they flow into your present and spoil things. When I become troubled about having left my mother, my husband comforts me with a passage in Mark 14: "Jesus said, 'Let her alone; why do you bother her? She has done a good deed to Me.'" Stuart always says to me, "Did you do what you could?" I say, "Yes, I think I did what I could at the time." He replies, "Then Jesus says that's enough."

Stuart Briscoe

I look back at many years of ministry and recognize there have been times when I've not responded appropriately to people. There have been times when I've said things incorrectly or inadvertently or thoughtlessly or casually that have gone deep with others. In fact, recently a gentleman came up to talk to me and reminded me of something I'd said (or that he recollects I'd said) some time ago. Well, if I did say what he says I said, I'm horrified. When quoted back to me, I reacted with, "I don't think I actually said that because I'm not sure I believe it." These are the areas in which I have my regrets.

Michael Card

I think the thing I regret the most is the early days when I first started doing music. I was fairly successful early on and was really arrogant. Yet I suspect I'm a good enough hypocrite that I don't think people knew how arrogant I was. My hypocrisy was really working for me at this point! But I look back on those days and think, *Man, you were arrogant.* Back then I even justified it to a point of saying, "To be creative, sometimes you need self-confidence." The older I get, of course, the more that confidence goes away. The process becomes harder and harder to create when you don't have that confidence. But I think in the early days I was probably pretty arrogant, and I regret that.

If I Could Do It All Over Again

Nancy DeMoss Wolgemuth

There are two big things that gnaw at my inner person when I become reflective and still enough to think. One is that I haven't loved better, that I've often been demanding and censorious and critical of others and not as gracious and loving in receiving others as God has been of me. The second regret is time I've wasted, so many moments and hours, not living intentionally. It's not that I don't spend a lot of hours being productive, but in the course of any given day, how many moments are just frittered away, not used carefully and wisely? If I could go back and do it all again, I would like to be more intentional and more purposeful about how I steward the hours the Lord has entrusted to me.

POINT TO PONDER

Be careful how you walk, not as unwise men but as wise, making the most of your time, because the days are evil.
EPHESIANS 5:15-16

Dee Brestin

I regret being slower to see the deceitfulness of my heart because it affected a lot of relationships, but I'm so thankful I see it now. I heard a sermon called "Models of Manipulation." Martha was said to be a manipulator because she liked to use guilt and make sideways comments instead of speaking directly. I thought, *Hmm...I always thought those things were a good idea.* But they ruined relationships, and I now have those regrets. I'm glad I see that now, and my relationships are so much better.

Ravi Zacharias

It's impossible to live through life without regrets. One is not human if he or she has nothing to be sorry about. Lord Byron said, "Youth is a mistake, manhood a struggle, old age a regret." Because I was so fearful of my dad, I regret I never ever talked to him in personal terms. I wish I could talk to my father about his life, about his youth. I never did because my dad was a strict and austere man. Although I lost my parents early, I look back now and say it would have been wonderful to sit at the dining table and say, "Dad, tell me a little bit about your life and how you became what you became." Those days are gone. I can't have those moments. There are so many choices you make through life which I think you ultimately regret.

Tony Evans

My greatest regret is being too much consumed by ministry. I wish I had not been so. As important as it is, ministry can become a Martha and Mary thing where you spend so much time *for* the Lord that you don't spend enough time *with* Him. I might have avoided that regret if I would have started each day with the Lord instead of needing to find time for the Lord. I regret not showing more appreciation for the things that money can't buy. I try to do that now—things like going for a walk or just being with friends. I'm growing in my appreciation of the beauty of God's natural creation, undisturbed by our occupation. If I could go back, I would try to enjoy those things more.

Jan Silvious

I wish I had been more present in rearing my children. I feel I was there physically, but I was always looking for something else, always wanted to do something beyond just being a mother. I wish I had been more focused on that. That's easy to say after the fact because now I'm a grandmother. I'm a very good grandmother, but I think I was an average mother. So I would like to do that again.

James MacDonald

I wish that in the inevitable interpersonal conflict that attends to three decades of ministry, I had been swifter to hear, slower to speak, and slower to anger. I believe God has done that work in my heart. This is a lesson to learn slowly.

POINT TO PONDER

Everyone must be quick to hear,
slow to speak *and* slow to anger;
for the anger of man does not achieve
the righteousness of God.
JAMES 1:19-20

Bob Moeller

The regret that haunts me is quitting something when God had not given me permission to quit. As a result, my decision created a negative impact on my family in many ways: emotionally, financially, and geographically. At the time I justified the decision in my own mind, but I had not taken into consideration its impact on others, and particularly my own family. But when we pull back and consider we're to prefer others above ourselves, to love and serve others, to look to the interests of others and not just ourselves, that's quite a bit different. Then we realize that before we make a decision, we really need to consider who it's going to impact—and how.

Gail MacDonald

When I became a Christ-follower as a teenager, I was such a zealous Christian that I turned off my family. I regret that. Instead of telling them the good they *did* give me, I tried to convince them of the good they *hadn't* given me, to my great distress. It took them 15 years to listen to my husband, Gordon, and me spiritually because I had done so much damage. My parents eventually came to faith, but not until their sixties. Fortunately, they lived into their eighties, so we had some wonderful times as believers together. But as I look back, I realize I contributed to their wasting time, spiritually. I think this scenario happens to a lot of young Christians because we are like the cans on the bumper of a wedding car screaming, "Look out—here we come!" We come across like that instead of recognizing that other people don't need our brashness.

To be very honest, in the early years of my ministry, I sometimes failed to separate the biblical from the cultural. I'm thinking of the '70s when kids were letting their hair grow and we thought this was wrong. I remember a young man who began attending youth group at a church I was pastoring. The kid was kind of defiant. I finally took him aside and said, "Look, I don't like your attitude. I don't like the length of your hair. Get a haircut and fit in with the group or don't come back." He never came back. That was a mistake. I shouldn't have done that. A woman once came to John Wesley and said, "Mr. Wesley, your tie is too long." So he said, "Get a pair of shears and cut it to the length that suits you." She did. Then he turned to the woman and said, "Madame, your tongue is too long. While I hold these shears, would you please stick it out?" I think we have to decide if an issue is cultural or biblical. The length of a person's hair is not really the issue.

POINT TO PONDER

The LORD gives wisdom;
from His mouth come knowledge and understanding.
PROVERBS 2:6

Joe Stowell

I regret I didn't read more, didn't feed my mind more, didn't stretch my intellect more. I wish I could have slowed down and spent more time stretching my mind. I think I could have been a better leader, a better pastor, a better preacher.

Joni Eareckson Tada

I regret I was not more grateful: more grateful to my mom and my dad and my sisters. Gratitude, for me, is now just a way of life. I say thank you constantly to the many, many people who do all kinds of things for me: brush my teeth, brush my hair, give me sips of coffee, feed me lunch, empty my leg bag. I'm constantly saying thank you. But when I was growing up—especially when I was a teenager—grumbling and complaining were more the order of the day rather than speaking thanks. So, if I have any regret, it's that I did not try to cultivate a grateful spirit earlier.

❧❧❧

Parting Thought

It's time for you and me to empty our pockets—our souls—of all those regrets and it-might-have-been moments. They simply aren't doing us any good. In fact, the sagging weight of all that false guilt and negativity is slowing us down and holding us back. We'll talk more in the next chapter about what to do with our regrets, but let's pause here and listen afresh to the advice of Hebrews 12:1-2:

Since we have so great a cloud of witnesses surrounding us, let us also lay aside every encumbrance and the sin which so easily entangles us, and let us run with endurance the race that is set before us, fixing our eyes on Jesus, the author and perfecter of faith, who for the joy set before Him endured the cross, despising the shame, and has sat down at the right hand of the throne of God.

10

What Do I Do with My Regrets?

I should be dead by now. Really.

Thankfully, as a boy of 15, I underwent surgery for scoliosis, a curvature of the spine. Had my parents not opted for such a treatment, statistics say I wouldn't be alive today because of the crushing my internal organs would have received from the twisting of my own spine. If not dead, my torso would resemble something like the fictional *Hunchback of Notre Dame*.

The surgery was no minor deal. First, an incision was made from my waist to the top of my shoulders (about two feet long). After straightening the spine and fastening two metal rods (each rod about a foot long) into the vertebrae, the surgeon chipped tiny fragments off my hip and then carefully placed them along the vertebrae to create a bone fusion.

Recovery was slow. Every four hours I was rotated from my back to my stomach on a circular bed frame resembling equipment from a circus acrobatic act. After nearly two weeks of rotating bed confinement, I was informed that the next day would be "casting day," when I would get a plaster cast covering most of my upper body, allowing for near normal mobility. I distinctly recall the nurse warning me the night before. "Your incision is healing, and you'll likely feel an itching sensation tonight. Whatever you do, don't scratch your scar."

But what I felt that night was more than an itching sensation. It was an itching assault. An itching warfare. I scratched (bad decision). And the scars itched more. I scratched more. And the scars itched still more. At the height of this agony (I do not overstate the moment), it was all I could do to force myself to clench the tubular steel of the circular frame bed and quote every Bible verse I'd ever learned over and over. It remains the most awful night of my life.

Who knew a scar could cause so much pain?

Regrets are scars of the soul. We carry them around with us, and every now and then they itch. So we scratch them. We replay that thoughtless deed, that hurtful conversation. But instead of relief, we sense only a greater discomfort. Rather than let these memories go, we often escalate the trauma by further indulging our regrets.

What *should* we do with our scars when they assault us at night or in moments of tired reflection?

Scars, medical experts tell us, require regular and proper care (mine still itch or get occasional scabs). But what kind of care is there for scars of the soul? It's a question we put to our contributors. Just what *should* we do with our regrets?

Walter Wangerin

This is simple: Pray for forgiveness. Ask the Christ who fought the devil to come and speak to our regret. Invariably, the word the Lord brings us is, "Go and sin no more. I have forgiven you. Now go on. Get up. Go back to your life and be better than you were."

George Verwer

I read a long time ago that regret is the most subtle form of self-love. The temptation to regret comes the same way as any other temptation. What we need to do is readily embrace the gift of God's grace. A lot of people have had their lives filled with failure, yet they do really well at the end. We need to encourage one another with that. Regarding our specific regrets, God has forgiven us. He knows how to work things out for good, so we can't dwell on regret. We have to somehow move forward because it's a form of anxiety to dwell on our regrets, paying too much attention to ourselves. We need to claim God's forgiveness and grace and press on.

Anne Graham Lotz

We have to leave our regrets at the cross. When regrets come that bring tears, lay them down and ask God to redeem them. He's the Redeemer. I love that name. He can redeem the years the locusts have eaten. He can redeem our failures. I've seen Him do that. He can bring glory out of brokenness, beauty out of ashes, and life from death. Revelation 21:5 tells us God makes everything new. There will be no more scars and no more memories of failure and regrets. He's going to make it all new.

Dee Brestin

We need to *talk* to our souls instead of *listen* to our souls. In Psalm 42:5, David asks, "Why, my soul, are you downcast? Why so disturbed within me? Put your hope in God" (NIV). Jesus paid for our sins in full, so we need to remind our souls of that, and we also need to learn from our regrets. When my husband was dying of cancer, he didn't want me to cancel all of my speaking engagements and, in retrospect, I wish I had. We didn't know how long he had to live. But then, within the next two years, my mother became very frail, and I thought, *I am going to be at her side. I am going to learn from this regret and not let this precious time slip away.* We can learn from our regrets, but we mustn't beat ourselves up because it's all paid in full!

Kay Arthur

What do we do with our regrets? Now that's a question I can answer readily for two reasons. One, I messed up so much before I came to know genuine salvation at the age of 29, and it had great ramifications. Second, I am a perfectionist. I battle with, "I could have done it better, I should have, I wish I had, why didn't I?" This is where I must run to the open arms of my Sovereign God and all His promises and bring them to bear on my regrets. Also, I would add that we need to remember Satan is the accuser of the children of God (Revelation 12:10-11), so I have to stay dressed in His armor, rejoicing that He will make me "stand in the presence of His glory, blameless with great joy" (Jude 24).

Michael Card

There's a book called *Sacrament of the Present Moment.* The idea in the book is that Satan doesn't want you in the present. That's the only place you can meet with God, so Satan drags you into the past with your regrets. He also drags you into the future with fear. You have these regrets from the past, and Satan doesn't want you in the present. He wants you in the past feeling guilty for the things you've done. That's why we must confess and repent but then we offer them up. In Psalm 51, David realizes that all he has is all God ever wanted: his broken spirit and his contrite heart. All we have to offer is our foolishness, but God takes it and uses it. All of it!

> ### Point to Ponder
>
> Be gracious to me, O God, according to Your lovingkindness;
> according to the greatness of Your compassion
> blot out my transgressions.
> Wash me thoroughly from my iniquity and
> cleanse me from my sin.
> PSALM 51:1-2

Steve Brown

Satan is a liar, and he's the one who condemns. We need to tell him where to go, where he belongs, because Jesus has pronounced that we're forgiven. No power on the face of the earth will tell us differently. Sometimes I say, "Lord, I'm sitting here blushing and wincing. How could I have done that?" Sometimes He says to me, "You think you surprised Me? You think it's not covered? Don't you believe what you preach?" That's how we deal with our regrets. There are many things I wish I'd done differently. I wish I'd loved more. I wish I hadn't been so angry. I wish I'd been kinder and more merciful. But it's all forgiven. It's all covered. I'm clothed in the righteousness of Christ. It's part of our nature to go back and to feel the regrets and to wince at the people we've hurt and the things we've done, but each time we need to remember that Jesus said, "It is finished." When He said, "It's finished," it really was!

Nancy DeMoss Wolgemuth

The first thing we have to do is thank God for grace. Go back to the cross. Preach the gospel to ourselves and realize, "I am not the Christ. I am a sinner who needs a Savior—and thank God I have a Savior." I thank God He has not dealt with me according to my sins or as I deserve. The sum total of my life will not be about how well I performed, how well I lived up to my goals, or how successfully I overcame my bad habits or sinful patterns. When it's said and done, the sum total will be Christ my righteousness. He took my sin—He who had no sin—on Himself. He clothed me in His righteousness, and that is the only basis on which I will ever be able to stand before God and not be ashamed. Every day I have to preach that gospel back to myself and live in the constant conscious awareness that Christ is my life. He is my righteousness. He is my only hope in life and in death.

Jan Silvious

I don't like to feel what regrets make me feel because I can't do anything about them. I can't go back and undo how I parented. I can't go back and undo when I was unkind. In the physiology of the brain, when we revisit those memories, the same hormones are released in our bodies that were released back at the time of the particular failure. That's why we must embrace what Paul said. He who had murdered, he who had caused great grief to the church was able to say, "Forgetting those things that are behind, I press on" (Philippians 3:13-14, paraphrased). It becomes an actual process of "I choose to forget that failure." It doesn't mean it will ever leave my brain. I'm aware of it. But I choose not to dwell on it because it tears me up and makes me ineffective for what I face today. It's a choice.

POINT TO PONDER

I, even I, am the one who wipes out your transgressions for
My own sake, and I will not remember your sins.
ISAIAH 43:25

James MacDonald

Romans 8:1 says, "There is now no condemnation for those who are in Christ Jesus." I believe all of our sins—past, present, and future—are under the blood of Christ, that we're forgiven. I think we need to live as forgiven people. Second Corinthians 7:10 says, "The sorrow that is according to the will of God produces a repentance without regret, leading to salvation, but the sorrow of the world produces death." Genuine repentance is not thinking about what I *should* have done or what I *could* have done. It's thinking about what *Christ* has done, and living in that. When your kids were little and they would act up, what you wanted was for them to forsake the bad behavior and go forward. That's what I believe the Lord wants for us. Not to wallow in our failures, but to revel in His grace and to give it to others.

Joni Eareckson Tada

I love to read passages in Scripture that remind me that God has a poor memory when it comes to my sin. He remembers my sin no more (Isaiah 43:25). He separates me from my sin as far as the east is from the west, as high as the heavens are above the earth (Psalm 103:11-12). That is what makes the Good News so great! God will not remember our sins. You know what? We shouldn't either.

POINT TO PONDER

As high as the heavens are above the earth,
so great is His lovingkindness toward those who fear Him.
As far as the east is from the west,
so far has He removed our transgressions from us.
PSALM 103:11-12

Michael W. Smith

You use regrets for good. That's one reason I started Rocketown, a club for kids in Nashville. I love speaking to youth. I'm able to say, "Hey, guys, let me tell you my story." Based on my own experiences, I have a little bit of credibility talking to some kid who is smoking dope every day and getting high, struggling with drugs. I say, "I've been there." He might respond, "Yeah, whatever." Then I tell him my story, and all of a sudden he's listening because I have been there. I get to say, "Guys, it's a dead-end street. It'll take you down. This is not what your destiny is." Regret gives me an opportunity to speak into kids' lives because of the fact that I've been there.

Joe Stowell

One thing we can't do with our regrets is go back and reverse them. They are what they are, and they are what we chose to do. I think one of Satan's great strategies to defeat us or take us down is to continue to accuse us of the things we have done wrong. One of the liberating things Jesus Christ brings to us—and it doesn't make any difference how bad it was or how deep it is—is His cleansing blood. The day is coming when there will be no more death and no more dying, and He will wipe away every tear and every sorrow about every regret. We will remember them no more. We will be ushered into eternity in His presence, where in the place of these regrets will be the eternal joy of being in His fellowship without hindrance, without the possibility of ever failing again. *That* is the benefit and the reward of knowing Christ as our Savior.

Parting Thoughts

Is it really possible for us to learn to see past our scars and to stop allowing them to define us? I think I found the answer in the belly of a ship.

Several years ago, my wife and I spent a week onboard the *Africa Mercy*. At 16,572 tons, the *Africa Mercy* is currently the largest charity hospital ship in the world. Operated by Mercy Ships, the *Africa Mercy* is staffed by volunteer doctors and nurses who pay for the privilege of donating their medical skills.

My time onboard was spent recording interviews and stories for Moody Radio listeners while also acquiring video footage for use by Mercy Ships. We spent many hours below decks observing surgeries in the operating rooms and visiting patients in the hospital wards.

On the first day, in a hallway I passed a teenaged girl whose face conjured up images of the horrifically scarred Freddy Krueger movie character. I confess that the sight was unsettling. I might have mumbled a hello to her. I don't recall. But the next day I saw her again. This time I consciously chose to say hello to this poor girl, whose face and upper body had been severely burned by a fire in her hut, caused by a kerosene lamp. She was onboard the *Africa Mercy* for a series of multiple plastic surgeries.

As most of my time was spent visiting patients and doctors, and observing surgeries, I saw much of this girl in the hallway. I waved, and she waved back. I smiled, and she did the same. Our passing each other became routine with friendly greetings. By the time the week was up, I can honestly say I knew her more as a friend than a patient with severe burns. In fact, I almost ceased to notice her scars. We were just fellow passengers in the same floating neighborhood tied to a wharf in Monrovia, Liberia. When I got to know the *person*, I stopped seeing the scars.

But what about when scars are of your own making? When you can't bear to look at your own face in the mirror for the scars you yourself created with ugly words or choices you made in the past. What then?

It's time for you to stop looking at *you*—and your scars. It's time, instead, to lock eyes with the Christ of Scripture who walked our hallways so He could redeem us and become our ultimate Friend. Through His sacrificial death on the cross, He gives us the ability to live better than a life of guilt and self-indictment. Is Christ your Savior? The Bible says there is no condemnation now (Romans 8:1)! He no longer sees our sins—yours or mine. Why waste time and emotional effort remembering something as ugly as a scar? It isn't there anymore! Regrets do *not* represent your destiny. Christ already sees you as righteous. Let's move out and move on in the strength of Jesus Christ, our righteousness.

11

One Thing I Can't Wait to Do in Heaven

A trip to Florida—in winter? For my wife and me, lifelong survivors of Illinois blizzards, this was a big deal. Just batting around ideas for our getaway made us feel sunny on the inside. Call it anticipation.

In one of those strange moments proving that husbands and wives who presume to really know each other are only fooling themselves, my wife announced she wanted to take a ride on an airboat (this from a woman who shows white knuckles when most anyone other than herself is behind the wheel of our car).

So we scoured the web and settled on a tour company run by "Gator Bruce," a story all in himself. We tried to envision what the sensation would be like—the humid swamp air blowing in our faces, the splash of the gators diving into the water. Anticipation! Would we sense terror or simply an appropriate level of respect for these deadly creatures?

The more we dreamed and planned for this outing, the greater our anticipation grew. And in case you're wondering, the trip did not disappoint. In fact, it was better than advertised—way better!

On a much grander scale, this is what heaven will be—way better than advertised. So...where is our sense of anticipation for heaven? Most of us ponder very little on eternity. Puritan Richard Baxter asked, "Why are not our hearts continually set on heaven? Why dwell we not there in constant contemplation? Bend thy soul to study eternity, busy thyself about the life to come...bathe thyself in Heaven's delights." I invite you now to "bend thy soul to study eternity" as others share their thoughts on "One thing I can't wait to do in heaven..." It's a great lesson on anticipation!

$$\backsim\backsim\backsim$$

Jill Briscoe

I want to meet Peter's wife. I wrote a book about her. I feel as though I really relate to her. God walked into her life, walked off with her husband for three years, and never apologized. Imagine their conversation:

PETER: I'm going now.

WIFE: Well, when are you coming back?

PETER: I don't know.

How did she manage? This little homespun Galilean girl—how did she cope without the breadwinner? Actually, an epistle tells us she was with Peter in his travels after the resurrection. I realized she faced some of the challenges (and many more) I have faced. She was a blessing to me, so I want to find her in heaven and say, "Thank you."

POINT TO PONDER

He will wipe away every tear from their eyes; and there will no longer be any death; there will no longer be any mourning, or crying, or pain; the first things have passed away.

REVELATION 21:4

Steve Brown

I would like to talk to C.S. Lewis. I want to sit with him and ask, "Dr. Lewis, you didn't really say that, did you? What did you mean when you wrote that? And did you ever feel that the Holy Spirit was talking through you and that you would touch the life of this old cynical preacher?"

Anne Graham Lotz

Of course, I want to see Jesus first! Then I want to meet some of those Old Testament characters. I want to meet Daniel, I want to meet Jeremiah, I want to meet Ezra. After that I want to be in a Bible class Jesus teaches, having Him open our mind to understand the Scriptures. Can you imagine? I would love to be taught the Scriptures by the Lord Jesus Himself with the kind of understanding He would give. I'm hoping we will have that opportunity.

Nancy DeMoss Wolgemuth

Let me say this. I'm really happy we won't have any email in heaven! I'm looking forward to being free from the task-oriented, task-driven existence many of us choose to live down here on earth. I'm hungry to focus more time—in fact, all of eternity—on pure-hearted worship: loving the Lord, honoring Him, and blessing Him. These are things we ought to be doing down here, but in our weak, fallen, frail human bodies we get distracted. I'm looking forward to being free in heaven to focus on the things—THE thing—the one Person who matters most.

POINT TO PONDER

There will no longer be any curse;
and the throne of God and of the Lamb will be in it,
and His bond-servants will serve Him.
REVELATION 22:3

Walter Wangerin

Right now, I don't truly know what heaven is. But I know this—and it's the *only* thing of which I can be sure—when I die I will be with Jesus. What that means in terms of experience or the world or even what heaven is like, I don't know. But it doesn't matter. Even as on earth, Christ is first among everything, and this I know: I will be with Jesus.

Michael Easley

One thing I cannot wait to do in heaven is entirely selfish: have a pain-free life. Because of a bad back, I live with chronic pain. I have a bad attitude. I have an ornery disposition. When you live with chronic pain, you wake up with it, you go to sleep with it. It ebbs and flows. That new body is sounding really appealing! I want to wake up, as one of the songwriters said, "breathing celestial air." I'm looking for a celestial spine that the pain no longer traverses up and down at unpredictable rates and speeds. It's very selfish, very petty, but that's the first thing that comes to mind.

Gail MacDonald

After seeing the Lord and all my family, I want to stand in line and see all my book mentors. I never knew one who walked around in my lifetime. So I'll probably start with Hudson and Maria Taylor, Mary Slessor, Amy Carmichael, Sarah Edwards, Jonathan Edwards, E. Stanley Jones, and Ruth Graham— just to start. Those would be at the very top of my list.

Tony Evans

I want to see a replay—a video replay—of some of the great events of the Bible, like the opening of the Red Sea or the Jordan River.

June Hunt

I want to ask God to reveal to me all the times He intervened when I had no idea He was actively involved in my life, and then I want to thank Him. I want to say, "Thank You, Lord, for all You've done for me—for kindness and grace I didn't realize on earth I had experienced."

Kay Arthur

I think the first place we will find ourselves is flat on our faces! I have eternity before me, and I am going to do it all in a brand-new, immortal, incorruptible body! "See how great a love the Father has bestowed on us, that we would be called children of God" (1 John 3:1). Just think. The whole family will be together forever and ever and ever with the Father, the Son, and the Spirit...face-to-face! Think of all we'll learn, know, and experience as we cry, "Holy, Holy, Holy...Worthy, Worthy, Worthy."

POINT TO PONDER

A voice came from the throne, saying,
"Give praise to our God, all you His bond-servants,
you who fear Him, the small and the great."
REVELATION 19:5

Ron Hutchcraft

I want to see Jesus. I suppose gold streets will be nice and also the gates made of all those precious stones, but I'd like to make a beeline for Jesus. He will still have the nail prints in His hands and feet. That's all He brought back from His time on earth—nail prints. The scars will still be there too. The old song says, "I will know my Redeemer when I reach the other side by the print of the nails in his hands." I look forward to worshipping Him in person and being overwhelmed by Him and joining a hundred million angels. The Bible describes ten thousand times ten thousand who are still in awe of Him, and they are with Him every day!

Tim Keller

I can't imagine what heaven is like. It's just beyond my ability. I don't think I would formulate my reaction as, "When I get to heaven, there's something I want to do." Your love relationship with the Triune God and with everyone around you will be perfect. Heaven is a world of love. Think about the moments in your life—the two or three moments where you felt the most loved, the most delighted, the most blissful, and the most over-the-top. Then multiply that by three billion. This must be what heaven is like.

Erwin Lutzer

Of course, the one thing I can't wait to do in heaven is to fall at the feet of Jesus. But having done that, the very next thing I would do is connect with those I knew on earth. My mother died at age 103, and people asked her, "Do you want to see your husband?" She said, "Oh, yes, I want to see my husband." Then she added, "But I really want to see Jesus!" I think that here on earth I am intrigued with the question, What are people like in heaven? How do you recognize them? They do not yet have their permanent bodies. But I take it that the soul takes on the characteristics of the body so that you can communicate with them. Even among those of us who contemplate heaven, a lot of mystery is involved.

James MacDonald

I want to sing! The great joy of my life is the worship services of our church. I'm not a good singer, but I love to join my voice with the Lord's people in our church and worship the Lord. I believe the endgame is worship. Preachers are going to be out of work in heaven. Worship leaders will have a chance to work there. And when we begin to sing—all of us from every tribe and tongue and nation, from every generation, from all over the earth—and bow before the Lord together, how awesome is that going to be? I can't wait for that!

POINT TO PONDER

Worthy is the Lamb that was slain to receive power and riches and wisdom and might and honor and glory and blessing.
REVELATION 5:12

Josh McDowell

I want to talk to the leper described in Mark 1. I want to know what caused him to come to Jesus, where he could have been killed at any moment. The leper's bold risk is one of the greatest things I've ever encountered. He came to Jesus and prayed the most pathetic prayer recorded in the Scripture. He said, "If thou wilt, thou canst make me clean" (1:40 KJV). He didn't doubt the power of Christ. He didn't say "If You *can*..." He said, "If You *will*, You can make me clean." He doubted the compassion of Christ, not the power of Christ. What was it that caused him to come?

Then I want to interact with the apostle Paul and then talk with Jesus!

Bob Moeller

One thing I can't wait to do in heaven is thank people. There are so many people I am so grateful for that God put in my life as a youngster, as a high school student, as a college student, seminarian, young pastor. There have been people in my life who have been such a gift from God, and I don't know that I ever adequately thanked them. I don't know if I ever told them how much they meant to me. So many of those people are gone now. But one of the things I really look forward to in heaven is thanking people for the way they loved me with the love of Christ, for the way they believed in me, invested in me, endured me, stayed with me, and gave of themselves. There are many people to thank. I'm grateful that even though in this life we are separated, there will be a chance to do that.

Harold Sala

I want to sit at the feet of Jesus. Sit at the feet of Jesus! I have a lot of loved ones who are there—a host of friends. I keep a prayer journal every day. Several years ago I started writing the names of men who were in school with me (fellow pastors and so forth) or dear friends who have preceded me. I'm on the third page of that journal. But how wonderful it will be to stand in the presence of the Lord and hear, "Well done, thou good and faithful servant."

Michael W. Smith

I want to make some music! Join in with the angels! I wonder what that's going to be like. I think colors are completely different up there. I think notes are different. It's probably just going to blow my mind. To be able to join in with whatever is sung in heaven is going to be on the wish list for me, and I have a feeling it's going to happen!

Joe Stowell

The person I most want to see in heaven is Jesus. That's certainly true. But then, because I really don't know in detail what heaven will be like, I think about meeting other people. When I grew up, I was an avid New York Yankees fan, and Mickey Mantle was my hero. I tracked his life after baseball, and he had a horrible struggle with alcoholism. Yet I heard that in the hospital, just before he died, he accepted Christ. I couldn't believe it! So maybe, after I bathe myself in the joy of fellowship with Jesus, I might look for Mickey—and get his autograph.

Joni Eareckson Tada

Most people assume I will jump up and dance and kick and do aerobics and be so excited about my new glorified body. My goodness, how wonderful it will be to have a body with hands that work and feet that walk and knees that bend, and a back that arches and hands that can be lifted high. But I think what I am most looking forward to in heaven is having a new heart. I cannot wait to feel—I mean, really feel—what it's like not to have a sinful thought, a rebellious inclination, a tendency to pity myself, or growl or grumble or complain. I can't wait to see what it feels like to have a heart free of sin. That will be heaven for me.

Parting Thought

Wow! What a journey we have been on, you and I. We have probed the hearts and minds of some of America's best-loved teachers, preachers, writers, and musicians. They have shared candidly, in many cases with a transparency that can only be described as courageous.

On the one hand, I found it refreshing—even reassuring—that my favorite Christian leaders struggle with many of the same issues that nip at my heels. It's nice to know they are human too, after all. On the other hand, I'm convicted by the lack of progress in my own spiritual journey.

Speaking of journeys, that reminds me of the fictional journey of Ebenezer Scrooge in Dickens's *A Christmas Carol*. It was not enough for the miserly Scrooge simply to travel to Christmas Past, Present, and Future. It was not enough merely to eavesdrop on conversations packed with wisdom. He needed to *change*, to *apply* all that wisdom;

hence, his visit to Bob Cratchit, and his announcement of a raise for Bob. Further evidence of Scrooge's transformation was his assistance to Tiny Tim. Dickens tells us the former penny-pincher became a generous second father to Tim. The changes in Scrooge's conduct were the evidence of his applied wisdom.

What about your own life journey? Will it be shaped by the wisdom we've just read? Will we merely consume it as information, or will we allow it to soak in for authentic life transformation? The availability of wisdom has nothing to do with whether or not that wisdom is applied! The story of Rehoboam in the book of 1 Kings offers disturbing evidence. He had wisdom—and plenty of it—but failed to act upon it.

Rehoboam, son of the world's wisest man, stood poised to become king in his father's place. But there was trouble throughout the northern tribes. Jeroboam, a capable administrator under Solomon, said this to Rehoboam:

"Your father was hard on us, like a heavy yoke. But if you'll lighten our load, I can persuade all of Israel to support your kingdom" (1 Kings 12:4, paraphrased). The unstated implication seems to be there would be big trouble if changes weren't made.

Rehoboam received similar counsel from the older men who had served his father, Solomon. They suggested that Rehoboam act graciously toward these tribes of Israel requesting relief.

But the arrogant Rehoboam rejected all this wisdom by taking an even tougher stance with the people. The results were devastating. The kingdom split, with the northern ten tribes spiraling downward into a spiritual rot as not one of their kings followed after God! Judah, too, descended into decay, and the world has never again seen the kingdom united.

None of this tragedy needed to happen. Why did it all go so wrong?

Please note that Rehoboam did not lack access to wisdom. His father, Solomon, was the wisest man who ever lived. Clearly, there was good counsel available from Solomon's advisers. Surely Rehoboam knew there was wisdom to be found in going to Yahweh Himself.

The key: Rehoboam *collected* good wisdom but failed to *act* upon it. He heard what was right but failed to do the right thing.

You hold in your hands the collected wisdom of a remarkable group of Christian leaders. It's one thing to read their words, to hear their advice. It's quite another for us to act upon that wisdom. May God Himself help us be "doers of the word, and not merely hearers who delude themselves" (James 1:22).

About the Author

Jon Gauger is...

- A cohost of two nationally distributed weekly radio programs:
  - *The Land and the Book,* heard weekly on 380+ outlets
  - *Reason Why,* heard daily on 200+ stations
- Heard daily as the announcer for the nationally released broadcast *Today in the Word,* weekly on Moody Presents, and also on Moody Radio's *Praise and Worship* Internet channel
- Award-winning narrator of more than 35 audiobooks
- Writer and voice of a weekly commentary aired nationally on Moody Radio
- Host of Jongauger.com website, updated weekly with Jon's *Thursday Thought* (blog)
- Member of the Jerry Jenkins Writers Guild

Jon is also an ordained minister and a seasoned communicator who has taught nationally and internationally. He is married to Diana—a great adventure partner. They are parents of two grown children and four grandchildren. Jon's travel adventures have taken him to more than 35 countries, where he has interviewed, photographed, and videoed subjects and stories ranging from AIDS to human trafficking, poverty, and persecution.

If you enjoyed this book, subscribe to Jon Gauger's *Thursday Thought.* This inspiring weekly blog comes to you as an email you when you sign up at Jon gauger.com.

Visit doitalloveragain.net for video trailers, audio excerpts, and more.

To learn more about Harvest House books and
to read sample chapters, visit our website:

www.harvesthousepublishers.com

HARVEST HOUSE PUBLISHERS
EUGENE, OREGON